BROTHERLY FAITHFULNESS

COMPANION VOLUME:

Brotherly Community
The Highest Command of Love
(Two Anabaptist Documents
   of 1650 and 1560)

By Andreas Ehrenpreis and
   Claus Felbinger

Introductions by Robert Friedmann

BROTHERLY FAITHFULNESS

Epistles from a Time of Persecution

by
Jakob Hutter

Martyred in 1536

PLOUGH PUBLISHING HOUSE
Hutterian Brethren
Rifton, New York
Robertsbridge, UK

Translated in 1979 by
The Hutterian Brethren
Rifton, New York

1st printing Aug. 1979
2nd printing Nov. 1979
3rd printing Feb. 1986

Library of Congress Cataloging in Publication Data

Huter, Jacob, d. 1536.
   Brotherly faithfulness epistles from a time of persecu-
tion.
   Consists mainly of the author's letters translated from
the German in various sources, including Fischer's
Jakob Huter (1956), and Wolkan's Geschicht-Buch der
Hutterischen Brüder (1923).
   Bibliography: p. 225
   Includes index.
   1. Huter, Jacob, d. 1536   2. Anabaptists—
Czechoslovakia—Moravia—Correspondence.
3.   Hutterite   Brethren—Czechoslovakia—Moravia—
Correspondence.   I. Title.
BX8143.H86A4 1979   284'.3   79-15886
ISBN 0-87486-191-8

Printed at Friesen Printers, Altona, Manitoba, Canada   3 286

Dedicated to all those faithful brothers and sisters who throughout the centuries have given their lives for Jesus and His Church community.

CONTENTS

Preface	xi
Introduction	1
Letter I	5
Letter II	13
Letter III	49
Letter IV	65
Letter V	75
Letter VI	103
Letter VII	119
Letter VIII	137
Letter IX	159
Appendix A: Jakob Hutter, c.1500-1536	185
Appendix B: Historical Background to Letter II	205
Appendix C: Authorship of Letter IX	219
Appendix D: The Hutterian Stand on Marriage and Divorce	221
Bibliography	225
Index	227

Our faith is not merely forty years old, nor was it invented by Jakob Hutter or anyone else. It was created by Jesus Christ, our Lord and Savior, and is contained in the teachings and writings of His holy apostles.

The Hutterian Chronicle, 1547

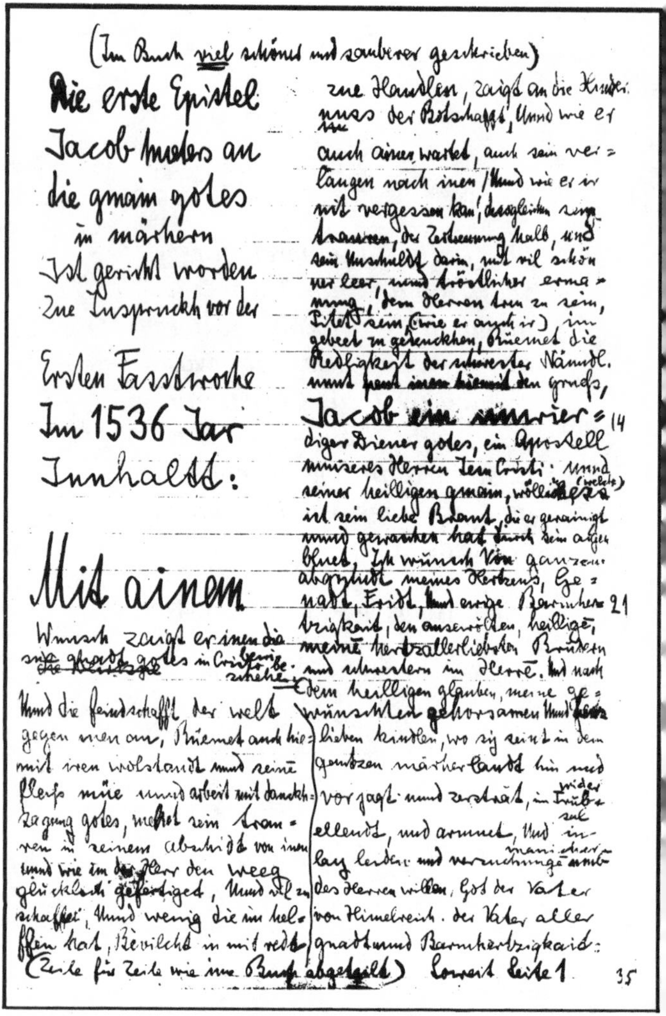
(Im Buch viel schöner und sauberer geschrieben)

Die erste Epistel
Jacob Huters an
die gmain gotes
in märhern
Ist geschickt worden
zue Auspitz vor der
Ersten Fastwoche
Im 1536 Jar
Innhaltt:

Mit ainem
Wunsch zaigt er inen die gnad gotes in Cristo beschehen
Und die feindschafft der welt
gegen inen an, Rüemet auch hiemit iren wolstandt und seinē
fleiss müe unnd arbeit mit danck-
sagung gotes, meldet sein trauren in seinem abschid von inen
unnd wie im der Herr den weeg
glücklich gefertiget, Und vil zu
schaffen, Und wenig die im hel-
ffen hat, Bevilcht in mit redt

zue Handlen, zaigt an die Kinder-
nuss der Botschafft, Und wie er
auch ainer wartet, auch sein ver-
langen nach inen, Und wie er ir
nit vergessen kan, desgleichen sein
trauren, der Zertrennung halb, und
sein Unschuldt darin, mit vil schön
ner leer, unnd tröstlicher erma-
nung, dem Herren treu zu sein,
Bitet sein (wie er auch ir) im
gebeet zu gedenckhen, Rüemet die
Redligkeit der schwester Wändl.
unnd peut inen hiemit den gruess,
Jacob ein unwier- 14
diger Diener gotes, ein Apostell
unnseres Herren Jesu Cristi: Unnd
seiner heilligen gmain, wölliche
ist sein liebe Braut, die er gerainigt
unnd gewaschen hat durch sein aigen
bluet, Ich wünsch Von gantzem
abgrundt meines Hertzens, Ge-
nade, Fridt, Und ewige Barmhertz- 21
zigkait, den auserwölten, heilligē,
meinē hertzallerliebsten Brüedern
und schwestern im Herrē. Und nach
dem heilligen glauben, meine ge-
wünschten gehorsamen Und
lieben kindlen, wo sy seint in dem
gantzen märherlandt hin und
vorjagt unnd zerstraet, in widerwärtigkeit, Trübsal
ellendt, und armuet, Und in
manicherlay leiden und versuchungē umb
des Herren willen, Got der Vater
von Himelreich. der Vater aller
gnadt und Barmhertzigkait:

(Zeile für Zeile wie im Buch abgeteilt) Lowreit Seite 1 35

First page of Eberhard Arnold's copy (see p. *xii*).

PREFACE

The urge to "live together in a world falling apart" has founded many communities in the last ten or twenty years. Many have failed, but the urge lives on—the search for lasting brotherly community. The need is for brotherly faithfulness, for a way of life so deeply and firmly founded that it cannot be forced apart either by people's weaknesses or sins, or by the cruel persecution of the world's dictators.

The Brothers whom men call Hutterian built on rock, and their communal life has lasted for four and a half centuries and is still alive today. Over 23,000 Hutterites are living in 260 communities in the United States and Canada.[1] It is with a deep sense of gratitude and awe before this miracle of God that we publish this collection of letters. They were written by Jakob Hutter, the leader by whose name the Hutterian Church came to be known. The fire of his love for Jesus and his faithfulness in serving his Anabaptist brothers and sisters during the 1530s shaped a communal life that by the grace of God still exists today. (See Appendix A for Jakob Hutter's life story.)

[1] As of February 1979.

The fervor, even passion, with which Jakob Hutter loved his suffering and persecuted brothers and sisters speaks to all of us who are trying to live in Christian brotherhood in this cold twentieth century. His love for Christ burned in his breast as love for brothers and sisters. This moved Eberhard Arnold deeply on his visit to the Hutterian Brothers in North America in 1930. For over a year, Eberhard Arnold was away from his small Christian community in Germany, visiting the Hutterites. Quite independently of the Hutterites, the group that had gathered around him in the 1920s was already living in a life-style based on the original Anabaptist community life. On behalf of his Brotherhood, Eberhard asked the Hutterian Brothers if his community could be united with theirs, and when they found that he agreed with them on all important matters of faith, they gave their consent. He and his community were finally incorporated into the Hutterian Church on December 9, 1930.

In July 1930 Eberhard Arnold copied out by hand, at the Rockport Bruderhof, the whole of the first letter that Jakob Hutter wrote in 1535 from Tirol to the Church in Moravia (see pp. 75-101; for a facsimile of the first page of Eberhard Arnold's copy see p. *x*). He sent it home, writing with great enthusiasm: "Read the whole letter to all our faithful and beloved brothers and sisters as coming from me in my weakness to express my great love to you all."

Then on September 14, 1930, after the Elder Joseph Kleinsasser had signed a letter on behalf of all Servants of the Word in Manitoba recommending the uniting, Eberhard was asked to read this same letter of Jakob Hutter at the Rosedale Bruderhof. We include here Eberhard's own account of that evening.

About nine o'clock the request came up that I should read aloud to the Servants of the Word the first letter Jakob Hutter wrote to the Church in Moravia in 1535. Zacharias Hofer Vetter wanted me to read it to all at Rosedale Bruderhof who wished to hear it. In a few minutes the children's dining room could not hold all the people who came, so we moved to the big dining room, which immediately filled up because *everybody* came, about 170 people. The Servants sat with me at the front table, facing the room. Joseph Kleinsasser Vetter gave a short introduction.

Thus began the first real Church meeting I was permitted to hold in Manitoba (that is, in America), and I was reading one of the most important Hutterian writings I know. (I have sent it to you from Rockport.) I was intensely moved and read quickly, without adding anything and with strong emphasis on the most important passages. I got quite warmed up, as you might expect. Joseph Hofer Vetter from Maxwell cried out, "Isn't he full of fire and life!" The whole letter made a very deep impression on everyone there, and the

Servants of the Word discussed it with me for quite a while in front of the whole gathering. We were deeply moved by Jakob Hutter's love to his people, by his sober-minded yet intrepid courage in the face of death, by the apostolic power of his proclamation of the truth, by his gift of prophecy, and by his strong awareness of the eternal nature of his mission.

Eberhard Arnold was a scholar of both early Christianity and Anabaptism. He prized greatly the early Anabaptist writings he found preserved by the Hutterian Brothers, many handwritten codices dating from the sixteenth and seventeenth centuries. When the Brothers saw how much he treasured them, both for their spiritual content and their historical value, they very generously gave or lent him many of their most valuable manuscripts. Eberhard had great hopes of publishing many of them, but this was prevented by his untimely death and by the rise of Hitler and National Socialism, which throttled the economy of the little Christian community. We who are privileged to continue living the community life that Eberhard Arnold started are all the more grateful that we can realize a few of these hopes in the United States today.

One of the sources used for translating the present collection of letters is just such a codex lent to Eberhard by the Brothers. This is the only complete source available to us for Letter IX (see Appendix C) and contains five of the other letters as well. Secondly, we have gratefully used the collection by Dr. Hans Fischer, *Jakob Huter: Leben, Frömmigkeit, Briefe*, for the eight letters it contains.[1] These two sources supplemented each other. We also referred to Dr. Rudolf Wolkan's edition of the Hutterian Chronicle, which contains the complete text of two of Jakob Hutter's letters.

Translating these 450-year-old letters posed a certain problem. Words poured from Jakob Hutter's pen in a warm profusion that will have struck the hearts of his brothers and sisters, but this profusion, literally translated, falls strangely on modern ears. J.B.Phillips writes in the foreword to his translation of the New Testament that there are three tests of a good translation. "The third and final test . . . is that of being able to produce in the hearts and minds of his readers an effect equivalent to that produced by the author upon his original readers." It was the challenge of this third test that gave us the courage to simplify Jakob Hutter's language in an attempt to capture the meaning and spirit of the original. The translators' problem was how to find the right balance between simplifying the language and keeping the original flavor.

We have chosen to spell the names of people and places consistently throughout the letters, using as our guide *The Mennonite Encyclopedia*. The Bible passages cited in the margin are largely supplied by

[1]Dr. Hans Fischer, *Jakob Huter: Leben, Frömmigkeit, Briefe* (Newton, KS: Mennonite Publication Office, 1956), used by permission of the Mennonite Historical Society.

the translators as indicated by Hutter's own words. Jakob Hutter and many other Anabaptists of his day were so much at home in the Scriptures that almost every thought had its root there.

We have included some historical material, taken primarily from the Hutterian Chronicle. The letters of Jakob Hutter spring to life in all their warmth and vitality when we realize that they were written at a time when the brothers were being scattered and hunted down, imprisoned, tried, and put to death for their beliefs.

Our grateful thanks go to the many scholars who have researched Anabaptist history and Anabaptist writings. For this small book we are particularly indebted to Rudolf Wolkan, Josef Beck, Hans Fischer, Johann Loserth, and Robert Friedmann. Complete bibliographical information is given at the back of the book instead of in footnotes. We were also very grateful for the abundance of material in *The Mennonite Encyclopedia* and especially for permission to include as an appendix the article on Jakob Hutter by Johann Loserth.

June 1979   *The Hutterian Brethren*

INTRODUCTION

The epistles or letters translated in this book were written at a time of severe persecution for the Hutterites. If we keep this in mind as we read them, we can sense something of what they meant at that time.

Jakob Hutter writes with a burning finger into the hearts of his brothers and sisters. He speaks with the heart and to the heart. Robert Friedmann says he uses the word "heart" more than any other word in his letters.[1]

Jakob Hutter had an unbelievably difficult task in such a time of suffering: to establish an order for the Brotherhood entrusted to him and at the same time to work as an apostle. Most of the brothers and sisters lived in Moravia, separated by hundreds of miles from Tirol, where Jakob Hutter did his mission work. His

---

[1]Robert Friedmann, in *Mennonite Quarterly Review*, January 1960, p. 38.

work was probably all done on foot, under the greatest difficulties and constant persecution.

These letters are a heartfelt affirmation of the life of the early Church, kindled again in this time of the Reformation. They express a deep faith in the living Christ and in the Word of the Bible. The Spirit of Christ was clearly felt as a power opposing and opposed by the spirit of this world and the spirit of the Antichrist. Consequently everyone who was willing to be baptized had to be ready to die a cruel death.

As in the early Church, most of those who joined the Anabaptists came from the lower classes. They were moved to give up everything and to join the brothers who were given the name Hutterites. Considering that the lower classes at that time were not educated, it is astonishing how well-read they were and how well they could express themselves in writing. They were especially well-read in the Bible and in the epistles of their Shepherds, which were circulated and copied out again and again.

The Bible and these epistles were the world these persecuted people lived in. There was for instance one man, Peter Voit, who was imprisoned for years in a dark dungeon in Eggenburg, Austria, his legs so tightly bound in irons that gangrene developed and the mice ate his toes. In such distress, to know the Bible and the epistles of the brothers was a source of great comfort and strength.

Jakob Hutter died as a young man, probably between thirty-three and thirty-five years old. He was taken prisoner in South Tirol in 1535, and in 1536 he was burned alive at Innsbruck. Two things were especially offensive to Jakob Hutter: the Roman Catholic Church, and the bearing of arms. So his enemies mocked him by putting a soldier's hat on him (a hat with a feather in it) and leading him through the Catholic cathedral. They had already tortured him terribly by cutting wounds in his body, pouring brandy into them and setting it on fire. He was burned to death in the market place at Innsbruck on February 25, 1536. A government building there has a little balcony called the "Dachl" overlooking the square. That is where the upper-class people of Innsbruck watched the scene of his burning and mocked him.

Of all Hutterian letters, Jakob Hutter's epistles are probably the most important. They speak of life and death; they challenged all those who had given their hearts to Jesus to a renewed commitment. All Hutterian Anabaptists were aware that this commitment was a question of life and death, but that he who endured to the end would be saved. Yet the deepest motivation of these brothers and sisters was not to be saved but to hold on to the deep, burning love of Christ, which put new life into their hearts.

May 27, 1979   *Heini Arnold*

LETTER I

Letter I was written from Tirol shortly after Whitsun 1530, at a time when persecution was becoming severe. It contains news of brothers captured and imprisoned—a daily threat.

This letter was sent to the brothers and sisters at Austerlitz and Bucovic, two towns in Moravia. Jakob Hutter had united with the community at Austerlitz the year before (1529). Hundreds of miles of mountainous terrain lay between the writer and the destination of his letter—a long and dangerous journey for its bearer.

To the chosen, the children of the living God, my beloved and faithful brothers and sisters in the Lord by God's grace, the grace we all received from the victory won by our Lord and Savior Jesus Christ:

Through our faith in His Son, God has accepted us as children. He wants to do good to us forevermore, but we must hold to Him alone and grow constantly in His love; we must be found irreproachable in all godly things, in our obedience, in all the ways of Heaven, and in our whole life and conduct, so that our way of living does not hinder the Gospel of Christ. That is my plea to you all, my beloved children and fellow members in the Body of our Lord Jesus Christ. I wish you during my absence God's boundless grace, peace, and compassion. May He conquer and prevail in all of you. That I wish you from God the Almighty, through Jesus Christ. Amen.

1 Cor. 9:12

O you beloved and faithful brothers and sisters in the Lord (who were living at Bucovic and Austerlitz when I last saw you), my beloved brothers and helpers Georg Hän and Christel, as well as all those who help you in the service of the brothers and the entire Church gathered with you: the love of God urges me to tell you a little of how things are with us. I know you long for us all the time, and we also long for you. For to us you are like a living letter, written in our hearts by the Holy Spirit, who stirs and moves everything within us. I saw this Spirit at

2 Cor. 3:3

work while I was with you. Therefore I
bend my knees before the Father of all
mercy and pray that you remain confident
and obedient, and that your faith, love,
and hope continue to grow, to the glory of
His great Name.

So then, I will not leave you wondering
how we, your companions in the Lord, are
faring. We are doing very well, all honor
and praise be to the Lord forever. But the
suffering that has been the lot of all
believers from the very beginning has
come upon us too, and that is good for us.
Yes, we are in great danger, but that does
us no harm. Otherwise all men, or many,
would choose to be Christians—but suffering serves to sift them. There are many
who enjoy hearing the Word of God, but if
they have to suffer for the Word's sake,
they soon turn away and go back to the
world.

The godless are raging furiously wherever
they know that the believers are gathered.
Before long, the eagle will set out, taking
the wolf, the lion, and the bear with him to Prov.
destroy the work of the Lord and to tear ^28:15

the lambs of Christ to pieces. Just now the godless have again cruelly snatched away a faithful brother, along with two new believers. On Saturday night, eight days before Whitsun, we wanted to meet, but the lords of H. came with a crowd of bailiffs and surrounded the house.[1] There were only two brothers in the house, and the Lord helped one of them to escape. Someone had betrayed them, reporting that they had a hundred guilders in their possession. But when the bailiffs found nothing, they took the brothers and the owner of the house to prison and stole what money and other things they could find.

And so, dear brothers and sisters, we wait for what the Lord has in store for us. Intercede for us, therefore, that the Lord may protect us, and pray earnestly that the Almighty God may keep us faithful to the glory of His Name.

I also plead with you, dear brothers and sisters, to struggle through in faith and to

---

[1]This raid took place on May 28, 1530, at Enn in the Puster Valley, Tirol. (Eberhard Arnold, p. 58)

be obedient to one another in love. Ponder
in your hearts the voice of God that moves
among you daily. I know for sure that you _{1 Cor.}
do not lack any good gift, so I do not feel I ^{1:7}
have to write you a long letter. His _{1 John}
spiritual anointing teaches you daily; it is ^{2:27}
the truth and no lie. Therefore be true to it
so that you do not lose what you have
received from the Lord. I pray that each
one of you, my fellow members, may take
this to heart. Brothers and sisters, watch
and pray! Your prayer will be very much
needed. We ask for nothing more than
that our needs are supplied and we are
shown a way through so that we can stand
before God with pure and upright hearts
and can rejoice in His coming with our
whole being! Let us think of this, let me
remind you of it with my whole heart in all
humility. I do not lack anything—that is
not why I am writing to you.

I entrust you to the Good Shepherd.
May He pasture you where you will find
grass aplenty. May He lead you to drink at
the living fountain of His Holy Spirit.
May He let this river with all its streamlets
flow into your hearts, into the hearts of all

John
15:1-8

the children of God, so that you will be
found fruitful branches of Christ, the true
and living Vine. So I commend you to
God in Heaven and to His Word of grace.
May He reveal His holy work powerfully
in you through Jesus Christ.

Now, dearly beloved brothers and
sisters, we greet each one of you very
specially: you, my brother Kaspar, Georg
Hän, Christel, Hans Fleischhacker,
Lorenz, Hans Plattner,[1] those of you who
work in the kitchen, in the school, in the

---

[1] Of those listed here, Kaspar Braitmichel and Georg Hän were
appointed to the Service of Temporal Need on All Saints' Day
(November 1) 1538, at Schäkowitz near Auspitz. (Wolkan, p.
143) Lorenz Schuster was appointed to the same Service at the
same time, but there is no proof that he is the Lorenz whom
Hutter greets above. Georg Hän remained in the Service of
Temporal Need until his death at Pergen near Nikolsburg in
1569. (Wolkan, p. 330)

Hans Plattner and Kaspar Braitmichel were appointed to the
Service of the Word at Holitsch in Hungary in 1548. Soon after,
during the severe persecution, Hans Plattner and three other
brothers were sent to Poland and Walachia to find a refuge for
the expelled and homeless Church. (Beck, p. 183)   Hans
Plattner died "in the Lord, having passed through much distress," at the beginning of 1552 at Austerlitz. (Wolkan, p. 258)

"On February 27, 1573, brother Kaspar Braitmichel, an old
Servant of God's Word and of His Church, fell asleep in the
Lord at Austerlitz. . . . He was one of the brothers who had been
taken to the sea from Falkenstein or Steinabrunn but had
escaped at Trieste. . . . It was he who began the Church Chronicle." (Wolkan, p. 362)

bath house, in the weaving room, and in the bakery—yes, each child of God personally, also at Austerlitz—we greet you all from our hearts.

I, Jakob H., and Klaus B. and all the believers who are with us—we all greet you with the kiss of our Lord Jesus Christ and with His peace and embrace you with the arms of our hearts.[1] May the God of peace and love gain the victory in you to the glory of His great Name, through Jesus Christ. Amen.

From me, Jakob, your servant and brother in the suffering of Christ.

---

[1]Klaus B., a fellow worker of Hutter, may be the same "dear brother Klaus" who in Hutter's second letter is reported to have brought a group from Carinthia to Auspitz (see p. 18) and to have copied Hutter's letter for him (see p. 46). Nothing more is known about him.

LETTER II

Letter II was sent in November 1533 from Auspitz in Moravia to the Adige Valley in Tirol, carried by brother Peter Voit. Jakob Hutter had come to live at Auspitz a few months earlier, for the persecution in Tirol had come to a peak. Brothers and sisters were streaming to Moravia.

This letter points clearly to Hutter's call from God to lead the Church. It was written after a crisis had split the Church in Moravia. (See Appendix B: Historical Background to Letter II.) He challenges the members to continued wakefulness and urges them to leave Tirol and join him in Moravia.

Jakob, through God's grace and mercy a servant of our Lord Jesus Christ and of His holy Christian Church, set apart by God our heavenly Father and called to proclaim His holy Word, to reveal His mystery and magnificent riches in these last days before the glorious and terrifying coming of our beloved Lord Jesus Christ. Praise and glory to Him, and honor and

13

thanks from our whole heart on behalf of myself and all holy Christian Shepherds and Servants and all believers wherever they may be, for all His love and faithfulness, the signs and miracles He has shown and is still showing us daily. His holy Name be praised through Jesus Christ for ever and ever.

Grace, peace, love, faith, victory, and eternal mercy—these I wish you from the bottom of my heart. All the believers and children of God join me in wishing this for you, my dearly beloved and longed-for fellow members in the Body of Jesus Christ, all of you in the Puster Valley, the Adige Valley, and the Inn Valley, or wherever you are scattered for the sake of the Name of God. May He comfort and strengthen you all with the precious comfort of His Holy Spirit.

Most dearly beloved brothers and sisters in the Lord, there is so much I would like to write to you and talk to you about, but I cannot. And no letter can reveal to you what is on my heart, nor can I really satisfy the longing of my heart. I would so much like to speak to you face to face. My heart is filled with an overwhelming longing for you, as God in Heaven knows well and all the children of God who are with me here. I have written this to you twice before; this is the third time, and you will surely hear it again.

Now I will let you know how it is with us here. We cannot fail to do this, out of true and deep brotherly love. On the Thursday after the feast day of Simon and Jude we sent our beloved brothers Kuntz Maurer and Michel Schuster to you.[1] We took leave of them in a fitting manner, praying and calling on God earnestly with the whole Church that He might speed them on their way to you and back to us with great joy. Through them we let you know in detail, both orally and in writing, how we were faring here and how much had happened in a short time. We hope that through God's grace this message has reached you.

[1]Simon and Jude's Day is October 28. Michel Schuster quite possibly was the brother Michel who delivered Letter V from Tirol to Moravia.

I will now give you a brief account of what has happened since and what God has revealed further. The brothers will tell you more in detail about everything; they will be our living letter to you, and you can ask them any questions.

The day after the brothers left, to our great joy Peter Voit arrived with all those you sent with him.[1] We all praised and thanked God. Our hearts leapt with joy in the Lord, and we were flooded by His love.

I received the letters from Hans [Amon], Offrus [Griesinger], and the other beloved brothers with great joy, but they brought me sadness, pain, and sorrow of heart. My heart was shocked and I wept many tears, as God knows, when I read the letter from our dear brother Hans, my beloved and faithful helper. And even now

---

[1]Peter Voit was a missionary who brought a group of converts from Tirol to Moravia. He was seized in Austria in 1534 and imprisoned in a dark dungeon in Eggenburg. His legs were so tightly bound in irons that gangrene developed in his feet. Helpless, he had to suffer while the mice ate his toes. When he was released, he somehow reached the exiled Hutterians in Moravia who were themselves in dire need (1538) and living on the open heath. Both his feet had to be amputated. He lived for many years, until 1570. (Wolkan, p. 106; M.E. IV, p. 842)

I am writing to you with weeping heart and eyes—God is my witness—for I have learned how violently you are being persecuted. God has allowed those villains to gain so much power over you that they have again imprisoned dearly beloved brothers and sisters. They took Valt, the faithful brother who was so dear to me, and the beloved children whom I bore with labor and great anguish through the grace of God, Gredl, Christina, Rüpel, Stoffel, and also Zentz and others who had been imprisoned before and had given a witness to God.[1]

1 Cor. 4:15
Gal. 4:19

Many, yes, really all the children of God who are here with me are also very much shocked at this news, for I lost no time in telling them my great sorrow. We also came before God our Father with earnest entreaties for you, and you can be sure that we will continue to intercede fervently for you.

[1]Valt (Waltan) Gsäl and six other brothers were executed at Gufidaun (Tirol) in October 1533. They died, "mightily admonishing the people to repent, . . . and showing that no impure, false, idle, or heedless hearts can stand the test." One of their letters reports that ten brothers and sisters were still in prison, and they all desired to witness to the Lord with their blood. (M.E. II, pp. 607-608) This probably included the others named here by Hutter.

A few days later, more brothers and sisters and several children came from the Puster and Inn valleys. You know who they are; I cannot name them all. On the same day our dear brother Klaus arrived from Carinthia and brought with him seven people. They have all found the faith here, praise be to God. Soon after that, brother Peter Hueter arrived with twenty-four souls, and the day before eighteen souls had arrived from Hesse. So we reckon that in the short time of three or four weeks the Lord added more than one hundred and twenty souls to the Church of God, who were baptized and taken into the community. Everyone was welcome. Adults and children, all those who came from other lands as well as from your area, were welcomed here with great joy as we would welcome the Lord himself.

We thank God from our hearts for these new brothers and sisters, and we will continually praise Him for making us worthy to receive His children and to shelter and serve them. That gives us a deep and heartfelt joy in the Lord. We also know how wonderfully God protected them on their journeys by water and by land, and we cannot stop marveling and praising the Lord for all the messages and letters and for all the beautiful, loving, and comforting greetings you sent us by word of mouth and in writing. These I read and shared fully with the whole Church.

Your letters are a great comfort to all of us, a delight and joy before God. We are all very eager to hear from you and to talk about you. I cannot tell you enough how our hearts praise God for all you write and all you do through God's grace and power and mercy. It is beautiful and pleasing to the heart, it is like a garland of gladness and delight to me and to all God's children, making us inwardly leap for joy. When you write or speak to us, we receive it as coming from God; it is almost as though the Angel Gabriel had written it. This is how we have always felt and how we feel now again about the letters from Hans and all of you dear brothers and servants of the Lord.

It has moved us deeply to hear of those who have overcome, those who have testified to God's Word, faithfully keeping their promise to the Lord and sealing with their blood the holy covenant they made with Him. For this we all praise God's holy Name, extolling His majesty and giving Him the honor and glory that belong to Him many thousand times more than we can ever give. His glory is great and unutterable! His Name be praised for you and all the believers and for all the signs and miracles He has done and continues to do daily through Jesus Christ, for ever and ever. Amen.

We really needed this encouragement in our pain and sorrow. It was a timely help to us; the Lord truly came at the right hour. We are greatly grieved and distressed on your account, because you are being so terribly persecuted and destroyed and we are thus robbed of your fellowship. Yet we have to endure sadness and pain as long as body and soul are one, as we read in the Book of Job.

My beloved children, I want to tell you that on the day after the departure of our brothers Kuntz and Michel, on a Friday, we saw three suns in the sky for a good long time, about an hour, as well as two rainbows. These had their backs turned toward each other, almost touching in the middle, and their ends pointed away from each other. And this I, Jakob, saw with my own eyes, and many brothers and sisters saw it with me. After a while the two suns and rainbows disappeared, and only the one sun remained. Even though the other two suns were not as bright as the one, they were clearly visible.

I feel this was no small miracle; it was a sign from God, and there was surely a reason why He allowed it to appear. This much I can tell you, but what the Lord had in mind and wanted to show us by it He alone knows. To Him all hidden things are known, whether present or future, in Heaven or below Heaven, on the earth or below the earth. This is what I feel. May the Lord protect us from all evil and keep us holy, pure, and blameless until the end; that is my prayer to God.

Further, my chosen and dearly beloved children of the truth and of the living God, I want to tell you what else happened

among us here. On the first Sunday after
the brothers started their journey to you,
we assembled the Church about two hours
before daybreak.[1] I wanted to speak the
Word of God to them in view of the need
that still exists. I challenged the brothers
and sisters very seriously to be watchful
and in all things maintain the right
attitude toward God and toward all men,
friends and enemies alike, so as not to fall
into the error of rash judgments and hasty
talk. This has happened often and still
does, as we have noticed frequently. There
was very good reason for this warning, but
it would take much too long to tell you
about it. I was seriously concerned, for
through God's Spirit and wisdom I knew
of a good many things that were going on
in the community—things partially
hidden, not to the extent that they could
not have been discerned, but yet not
revealed in the Church.

As there are so many single brothers
and sisters here, I had in mind also to
speak about marriage, so that each one

[1]According to the Chronicle, it was October 26, 1533. (Wolkan,
p. 82)

might know how to bear his situation
better and how to take the right attitude. I
was concerned lest in speaking plainly
about the right foundation I might say too
much for some, and that they might seek
to find fault with my words and accuse me
or something like that. I was especially
afraid of Philipp and Gabriel, and not
without reason, yet I feared God even
more.[1] So I was prepared to speak the
truth with prudence and modesty, trying
to find the right and holy way, so that I
could stand before God and let neither
Philipp nor Gabriel nor any other man
intimidate me. The great need urged me
on, and I felt compelled by God's Spirit
and the fear of Him. And so with great
earnestness I pleaded with the people to
listen carefully to what I was saying so that
they could give a witness if needed. I spoke
in this way also for other reasons, which

[1]Three communities were living about twenty-five miles apart.
One at Auspitz was being led by Jakob Hutter and Simon
Schützinger, another (also at Auspitz) by Philipp Plener, and
another at Rossitz by Gabriel Ascherham. In 1531 they united,
agreeing that they would not make major decisions
independently of each other. For the cause of Hutter's anxiety
and a summary of the crisis that split the Church, see Appendix
B: Historical Background to Letter II.

soon became evident to all those who were present.

Suddenly, after I had spoken and we were all about to fall on our knees in prayer before God, Philipp and Blasius and Gabriel and Peter Hueter from Rossitz entered the room without our previous knowledge or agreement.[1] We welcomed them as brothers, although for several reasons their arrival was a shock to nearly all of us. We had never experienced anything like this before. Nevertheless I asked them to say what they had on their minds.

They began by appealing to God and declaring that they had come for the sake of peace and unity and in true love, and words to that effect. They made them-

---

[1]Blasius Kuhn was Philipp Plener's assistant. He had been won and baptized by Philipp in or near Bruchsal and in 1531 followed him to Auspitz with the remnants of the Bruchsal congregation. (M.E. IV, pp. 192-193)

Peter Hueter was Gabriel Ascherham's chief assistant at Rossitz and came with him to this fateful early morning meeting on Sunday, October 26, 1533. (Wolkan, p. 82) The Chronicle reports how four years after the unfortunate split, Peter Hueter came to the Trässenhofen Bruderhof on September 14, 1537, in order to repent. He accused himself severely because of his wrongdoings and mistakes and declared his readiness to turn around. (Wolkan, p. 134)

selves out to be peaceful messengers and angels of God; they came in sheep's clothing and with the appearance of angels of light. But inwardly they were ravening wolves, which do not spare the flock, as Christ and the Apostle Paul say. We easily recognized them by their fruits, their words, and their works, and with great power God revealed them before I had spoken one word about marriage.

Matt. 7:15
Acts 20:29

For this I praise God from my heart and rejoice mightily, because otherwise they would have tried to attack me on account of my words. Others may have thought that I brought up the subject specially because of them, which was not the case. But God no longer tolerated their evil and cunning; He did not want devout hearts to be deceived any longer, so He delivered them from the jaws of those whose poison had deceived them for so long. That is why God allowed the envy and hatred in their embittered hearts to be exposed before the whole Church here. Then they had to reveal the poisonous feelings they had harbored for so long. And the entire holy Church of God recognized them as liars, slanderers, and false shepherds. Therefore they were excluded by the Church and handed over to the Devil in the power, Spirit, and truth of God.

1 Cor.
5:5
1 Tim.
1:20
2 Tim.
2:25,26

Nobody should think that we acted lightly in this matter; there is no reason for thinking so. We acted with great earnestness and in the fear of God, according to God's command and to what is right and good before Him. We acted carefully and with wisdom and discretion, taking everything into consideration. We cannot help it that they take offense at what is good and right. That is exactly what the godless have always done to all the faithful since the beginning of the world. But woe to them for turning what is good into a reason for doing evil! Our conscience is free and clear before God and does not accuse us with regard to any part, large or small, of this whole matter. Nor did we deal with them rashly; on the contrary, we considered everything thoroughly, looking at it in the true light. For about five days we concerned ourselves with it in great pain and trembling before God, together with the whole Church.

We did not deal with them in a prejudiced way either. We did not bring up the difficulties that had frequently arisen before and about which a great deal could be said. (But now God and we hold them accountable for these matters too, because there had never been repentance or a real improvement.) We only spoke of what we actually saw and heard, nothing more. And all their accusations have been confuted by many faithful witnesses, in fact, by the whole Church of God.

It would take too long to tell how it all began, all the reasons for and details of what happened, everything that was said, and how it was finally settled. The brothers will report to you as much as they know and are able to tell. Besides, I am sure that it is not necessary to write it all down since I know you have a deep trust in me and in all of us. We all stand fully revealed to you in your hearts, and I hope you believe us as if God were speaking to you, which is right, for we do speak the Word of God.

Here is a summary of it all. We lived in great love, peace, and unity. The Church of God grew in all Christian works and virtues ever since we separated from those evil and deceitful people like Simon and others, who had once been so lovingly embraced by the community.[1] These false brothers had slandered and defamed us; all peace and unity had come to an end, and this continued as long as Simon had his way. It started as soon as I arrived here. In fact, without any fear of God they persecuted and slandered me and all of us more terribly than any unbeliever or cruel tyrant, any false prophet or false brother, has ever done. God knows this is true. Oh, what a big thorn in their flesh I am, even though I have shown them nothing but love from the bottom of my heart and stood by them faithfully as a true Christian. But they talk and shout so terribly against me that it is dreadful to listen to or tell about. They spread many horrible stories about me, saying that no greater

[1] Simon Schützinger (dates unknown) was born in Rattenberg in Tirol. He became Jakob Hutter's assistant in the late 1520s and accompanied Hutter on three journeys from Tirol to Moravia. In 1531 Schützinger had been appointed leader of one of the communities at Auspitz but had had to be excluded in 1533 because he and his wife had hidden money in their house. (M.E. IV, p. 485)

rogue than I has ever come into the land. They all clamor for revenge and wish me evil, and their greatest longing is that God might put me to shame.

They say that my coming brought division and disunity, that previously they had lived in true peace, and that I am the cause of their division. But I am comforted by the Lord, because an undeserved curse does no harm, and God does not hear the prayer of the unrighteous. I have done nothing to deserve it, I am not guilty of anything, great or small. God knows I did not come to break the peace and the unity but to increase them. This I began to do faithfully, and there are many honest witnesses who can testify to this. God has kept my heart pure and undefiled. In this whole matter there has never been any falsehood in my heart.

All the things for which they hate and revile me have come about through the Lord's great mercy. He alone is the cause. I will let Him alone answer for it; He has the strength and the wisdom. He has done it through me, His weak and miserable vessel; I myself am quite incapable of it.

Prov. 26:2
Prov. 28:9

But the many evil lies they spread about me, I bear and suffer gladly for the sake of the Lord and His holy people, and He helps me faithfully to carry it—otherwise I could not do it. They rage against me so terribly that words cannot describe it. I think they would like to stir up the unbelievers against me if they could, and we have already heard something to that effect from the judge here and from other sources. They say I bought the people's favor with money and that the people worship me on account of the money. They spread wicked, devilish lies like this, such as I have never heard before.

You can see that I am very much in need of your prayers, as we all are, so that God may protect me from their jaws. The Lord will surely do this; I trust fully in His great mercy. And even if He were to give them power over my flesh, and even if my soul were gravely threatened by them, still I am in God's hand. Christ and all the prophets and apostles were reviled and persecuted, so why should it be different with me? Yet only for the sake of truth and divine justice!

2 Tim.
4:17

They hate us all without any cause. And
everything that Simon, Gabriel, Philipp,
and others had planned to do to me has
come upon them. They dug a pit for me
and fell into it themselves (as the Holy
Spirit declares through David); the
righteous judgment of God was executed
upon them, just as it was on wicked
Haman; and while destroying others they
were destroyed themselves (as the Apostle
Peter points out). Their folly and villainy
is evident to anyone who is willing to see
and hear it. That is what the Apostle Paul
says about this end-time and wicked people such as these. That they are wicked has
been brought to light; it is no longer
hidden.

They still want to uphold Simon and
make him appear to be a faithful brother.
Me, however, they want to destroy. They
did all they could to support Simon with
human strength, but the Lord stood by me
in everything and helped me gain the victory. He does not forsake His own. Yet
right up to this day they believe Simon and
all other rogues and evil men more than all
of us. They welcome those whom we

Marginal references:
John 15:25
Ps. 7:15
Esther 7
2 Pet. 2:1,13
2 Tim. 3:1-9
2 Tim. 4:17

excluded for their sin and declare shamelessly that these are more trust-worthy than all of us put together.

O brothers, what a struggle has come over the Church of God! How we have had to wrestle with wild beasts! How much we needed to be armed with the spiritual weapons the Holy Spirit speaks of in the Scriptures! And if God had not stood by us with His great power, we would certainly all have been driven apart, scattered, and destroyed. But God gave us the victory, He has been our Captain; He has held us together like a strong wall and powerful fortress.

Several who were not deeply committed have left us; they had never been clear in any case and were never completely at peace with God's people. For a long time they looked for a reason to leave us; and now they have found it, we praise God that they have gone. All slack·and super-ficial souls must be eliminated from the Church through trials and suffering, just as dross is separated from gold by fire, and chaff from wheat by the wind. But those

Rom.
13:12
2 Cor.
10:3-6

1 Cor.
15:57

who are faithful and God-fearing have all
been kept together in love, faith, peace,
and unity, through the power and grace of
God. Many sincere Christian souls have
come to the Church of God to take the
place of the evil ones who left. This is to us
a sure sign that God is with us and that all
we have done or left undone is according
to the will and Word of God. We have
been faithfully upheld by His mighty arm.

O what a mighty storm, what a great
blow has struck the House of God! These
men had such a good reputation with most
people that no one could oppose them;
practically everyone had to bow and
scrape before them. Even though someone
might have had an uneasy feeling about
what they said and did, he would not have
had the courage to admonish them.
Whoever dared was no longer their friend,
that was quite clear. But anyone who
flattered them and said amen to all they
did or left undone, good or evil, was their
brother and dear friend. I could easily
have created this kind of unity with many
of them, but it would not have been from
God. It would have been sinning.

Rom.
10:2-5

There are many who have a zeal for peace and unity, but it is a misguided zeal. They do not discern God's way of righteousness, which brings about unity. They want to set up their own righteousness and what is good in their own opinion, but they are unwilling to submit to the righteousness that is valid before God. What the Apostle Paul said of the Jews is

Matt.
15:13

now true of many people. These plants are not planted by God and therefore cannot endure. However long we go on patching and mending, things will only go from bad

Matt.
9:16
Mark
2:21
Luke
5:36
2 Chron.
32:8

to worse, just like putting a new patch on an old garment. The arm that guided those people was a carnal one, but that which guided us was spiritual and powerful. God dealt with them with firmness, wisdom, and great power, so that they could no longer hide but had to reveal themselves and bring to light the deceitfulness of their hearts. Otherwise they would have continued to deceive us and to lead us around by the nose.

But God could not bear to look on any longer. He opened up things before our eyes in a marvelous way and with glorious power, and for that we cannot praise Him enough. The Devil could no longer conceal himself. He showed himself in a very crude way. But that was God's doing. I think they themselves now regret to some extent that they went about it in such a blunt and unwise manner. Had they been more subtle, we would not be rid of them yet and would have to put up with them still longer. But their hearts were stubborn and hardened. The evildoers we excluded are supporting each other in their wrong, and I fear that many or at least some of them may never come to true repentance. That is what I am afraid of, but I certainly do not want to deny God's grace to anyone. The way they have been so far, it is truly a lost cause; that is clear to me. Simon at first wanted to repent, but now he is worse than ever, maligning and abusing us in such a way that you might think he was a raging lion. Also David, Gilg, Marx, and many others are in every way much worse than before. But that is the fate of evil and unfaithful hearts. They are bound to be led astray and become hardened;[1] the Scriptures give many examples.

We tell you all this in true love and fear of God, as a Word from the Lord. We owe you this report so that you can be on your guard against these people and against all evil. Accept this warning for the sake of God's love and mercy, and lift your hearts and heads up to God, because the hour of peril, the very last hour, is at hand, as

1 John
2:18

[1]David Böhem (Bohemian David) had stood with Wilhelm Reublin and Georg Zaunring against Jakob Wideman in Austerlitz and was one of Zaunring's assistants in Auspitz. It was revealed that when moving from Austerlitz to Auspitz, he had bribed the magistrate of Nikolschitz into giving them protection from robbers on the trek to Auspitz without the other brothers' knowledge. When admonished about this, "he was not able to give honor to God in true humility but stood by his own opinions, and so was disciplined before the gathered Church." In addition he had helped Georg Zaunring to hush up the adultery of Zaunring's wife, an inexcusable action in the Church; later he became guilty of envy toward Zaunring and admitted it. Nevertheless, Gabriel and Philipp said he was treated unjustly by the Church. (Wolkan, pp. 67-68,71,72,86)

According to the Chronicle, Gilg Schneider was a Servant of the Word who led a small group from Hesse to Auspitz with Hans Both in September 1533. For a time they joined the group headed by Schützinger and Hutter. But the encounter was not a happy one. Because of basic differences in belief as well as insincerity and deceitfulness, Hans Both and his followers were excluded from the Church, whereupon they went over to the side of Philipp Plener whom they had previously declared to be in the wrong. (Wolkan, pp.101-102)

Christ and all the prophets and apostles foretold. Therefore wake up, for the Lord will come with great power and is not far off. Let each one get ready and arm himself with love, faith, patience, with righteousness, holiness, and truth, so that we may be found irreproachable before Him and have free and sure access to Him when He comes; then we will have joy and delight in Him with all the heavenly hosts. May God the Father help us toward this through Jesus Christ our Lord. To Him be praise and honor forever.

Luke 21:28
Rom. 13:11
1 Cor. 15:52

Eph. 2:18; 3:12

Rejoice and be comforted in the Lord, you holy children of the living God, for He is with us. He is our Captain and Watchman, our Power, Strength, and Shield. Praise be to Him eternally.

Ps. 144:2

I want to let you know, my dear children, my fellow members in the Body of Jesus Christ, that there is great love among us here; there is justice and truth, and the peace and unity of the Holy Spirit. Love to God and to our neighbor, the love we feel for one another, is increasing. The peace of God is flourishing and truth blooms, bringing forth many divine fruits.

God's children here are blossoming like beautiful flowers in the fields, which bloom when winter and the dark time is past, when summer arrives, and when gentle May rains moisten the ground and make everything fruitful. As we wrote you before, there is continual growth and increase on all sides.

Ps. 52:1-5

The Lord has taken away much power from the Devil, who constantly tried to hinder us. God will root him out of His holy Church, as we read in the Psalms of David. He is indeed doing this every day. Thorns such as these men are have always prevented the good seed from sprouting and bearing fruit. For the first time hearts and consciences are truly free from outward cares and human commandments, and the Lord has delivered them from heavy burdens. Many, not just a few, were bound by a human spirit and by the arbitrary commandments of men; their hearts and consciences had long been burdened, confused, and distressed by their false shepherd and other misguided people. All these Christ has set free. He took pity on them and led them out of bondage and is now walking ahead of them. And the lambs, the obedient children of God, all rejoice in His voice and His salvation, and they follow Him faithfully. They refuse to listen to the voice of a stranger, for they know and obey the [John 10:4] voice of their Shepherd and King. This King and Shepherd is Christ. That hurts and infuriates the Devil, making him roar like a raging, devouring lion. [Ps. 22:13]

My dearly beloved brothers, there is no doubt that the only freedom we can have is the freedom of Christ, not the freedom of the flesh. Only God can make us free, through Christ, and only the Holy Spirit can redeem our hearts. But our flesh can have no freedom or security anywhere. Still we are quite joyful and courageous, for we know that as our outer nature [2 Cor. 4:16] diminishes and decays, our inner nature grows and is renewed day by day. We also know that we have a dwelling place in [2 Cor. 5:1] Heaven, made not by hands but by the power of the infinite God—a habitation that remains forever and can never be destroyed like this mortal, bodily frame. And for this home we yearn with our [2 Cor. 5:2-4] whole heart; it is the goal of our longing, thoughts, and hopes. Toward this we strive, leaving behind this transitory life and everything that is of the earth.

Our hearts are full of joy. We exult in the Lord and thank Him for His goodness, faithfulness, and fatherly compassion, and for His redeeming presence. He satisfies our hearts, making us very quiet and still before Him. For this we all praise and glorify His most holy, all-powerful Name. We thank Him unceasingly with all our hearts for His goodness to ourselves and to you. We want to magnify and praise His Name and not silently pass over His wonders and deeds but proclaim them to all the faithful. Even among unbelievers we want to praise, thank, and honor the Lord and declare His wonders for ever and ever. His deeds are mighty, and He has done great things for us, for He is powerful and His Name is holy. His Name be magnified and honored by us and by all the believers and all the heavenly hosts through Jesus Christ, from everlasting to everlasting. Amen.

Heb. 2:12,13

Luke 1:49-51

You dearly beloved brothers and sisters in the Lord, I want to tell you that our greatest concern still is about you. It saddens our hearts deeply and causes us great pain and distress. Our hearts find no rest by day or night (God is our witness) because you are being persecuted and tortured with utmost cruelty and secretly murdered or suppressed. May God in Heaven have mercy! It wounds our hearts to the quick that you are being taken from us like this.

O dearly beloved fellow members, how we long for all of you, how much we suffer on your behalf, and what deep compassion and grief we feel for you! Our hearts weep for you constantly; they are heavy and sorrowful because of your suffering. Sometimes it seems as if they will melt away with the pain and great sadness, and that they are about to break. Because of you our souls have no peace or rest in our bodies; we just cannot find enough words to tell you how we feel. And we hear one sad and pitiful story after another. When I think of it, I feel more like weeping and crying my heart out than writing.

Now the Devil is destroying one brother after another. Oh, dear brothers and sisters, this fills all of us with great pity and compassion! If only my own person were involved, I would often rather die than hear such news. Every day and every hour we are in great fear for those of you who are still free, and every day we must expect to be told that you too have been captured. We know that our worrying does no good, and yet we cannot stop worrying, because of the childlike, brotherly love that burns in us. And though it helps neither you nor us and drains our strength and courage, it shows how deeply we love you and drives us to intercede for you by day and by night with earnest crying to God.

Well, I have written this to you twice already with my own hand,[1] and now I am

---

[1] This is the second reference in this letter to two earlier letters Jakob Hutter must have written to the Tirolean Church since his arrival at Auspitz in August 1533 (see also p. 15). These two letters seem to have been lost.

Hans Amon and Offrus Griesinger, who had continued Hutter's mission work in Tirol, acted upon his urgent call for the brothers and sisters to leave Tirol and take refuge in Moravia. The Chronicle reports that they arrived at Auspitz, bringing with them groups of refugee brothers and sisters from the mountains. (Wolkan, pp. 105-106)

writing you for the third time with tears and a weeping heart: we all urge you to come out of that accursed and murderous land. Flee, flee away from those godless and wicked people! Surely this is God's plan for you.

O that God might grant our prayers and protect you from their rage, those of you who are still alive and free. We long that He might send you to us. That would be our hearts' delight! If this were possible, we would all willingly endure hunger and thirst, cold and heat, and all kinds of suffering. If it were God's will for you to come to us, we would gladly be persecuted and driven out tomorrow. Oh, would to God that our prayers for you might be answered and that He might bless us by leading you to us. May God's will be done according to His holy compassion and goodness, and may He fulfill your and our heartfelt desire.

My dear children and fellow members, take heed of what I write to you and receive it well. For truth is confirmed by the testimony of two or three witnesses. 2 Cor. 13:1 Therefore be watchful and pray to God 1 Tim. 5:19

diligently. He will teach you what is right
if you will listen to Him.

Now I commend all of you to the
protection of God's mighty hand. May the
Lord be your Guard and Captain, your
Shelter and Shield, keeping safe your souls
and bodies until the great Day of the
Lord's revelation, through Jesus Christ.

The entire holy Church of God here, all
Servants and elders, all brothers and
sisters, whether old or young, greet you
earnestly from their hearts a thousand
times in truly burning and brotherly love
and with the kiss of our Lord Jesus Christ.
We greet all of you together and each one
personally. This comes especially from
those of us who know you so well and who
have a special love for you. I cannot pass
on with pen and ink every personal
greeting the brothers and sisters here
would like me to; it would simply take too
much time. But you know their hearts
well, for they are wide open to you in the
love of God. So please accept our
greetings, each one of you, and know them
to be a thousand times better than

anything I could write here. The brothers and sisters would have liked me to put down the name of each one, but I simply cannot.

And I, Jakob, your servant and brother in the Lord, an apostle of God through His grace, greet you all a thousand times from the bottom of my heart with the holy kiss of love. I think of you every hour and every moment. With my whole heart and mind and soul I am thankful for you. And I kiss you with my heart and mind, with the true kiss of Jesus Christ and of all the holy men of God. Although I am not with you in the flesh, my thoughts are completely with you all, and I cannot put into words how much my heart longs for you.

Give my greetings especially to all those who know me and who truly love me for the sake of the Lord. They are particularly close to me, and I love them with my whole heart. Brothers and sisters, Shepherds and sheep, in the Puster, Adige, or Inn valleys: greet each one of them. They are well aware of the faithful love I feel for them, even though I cannot mention each one by name. I wish I could still greet and comfort each one of you individually and kiss you with my own lips and heart. I wish I could serve you with my own hands and show you love with all my strength. That would be my greatest delight and give me joy in God.

My heart and mind are with you forever; your heart, soul, and spirit are with me, and may God the Father be with us all through Jesus Christ, from everlasting to everlasting. Amen.

I, Jakob, wrote this with my own hand, but Klaus has copied it for me, and we are sending the copy to the Puster Valley. If there is anything else you should know, brother Voit will tell you personally. Offrus [Griesinger] and Hans [Amon], I greet you faithfully from my heart. Please also give my warmest greetings to the dear sisters Gredl Marbeck and Ursula Brähl and to all the others. We have received Georg Fasser's wife back into the Church,[1]

---

[1]Ursula Fasser had been excluded for withholding money from the Church. (Wolkan, p. 80) Her husband Georg Fasser, a native of Kitzbühel in Tirol, was a close friend of Jakob Hutter and Jeronimus Käls. Though illiterate, he was a very active Hutterite missionary and was martyred in 1537 or 1538. (M.E. II, pp. 313-314)

through God's mercy and grace, and it goes very well with her, also Bärbl from Jembach. Your hearts will rejoice about this news. Georg Fasser, our brother and servant of the Lord, and his wife, our dear sister, greet you all very faithfully, and once again all the brothers and sisters here. The Lord be with you eternally. Amen.

LETTER III

Letter III was written in 1534 from Auspitz in Moravia to the brothers and sisters imprisoned at Hohenwart, Lower Austria.[1] To console and encourage them, Jakob Hutter reminds them of many passages from the Old Testament and the New Testament.

By this time, persecution had driven most of the Anabaptists out of Tirol, but it was increasing also in Moravia.

Jakob, a servant of Jesus Christ, with other servants and the whole Church of God, writing to those imprisoned at Hohenwart for the sake of Christ Jesus:

[1]Hohenwart is a parish in Lower Austria where Anabaptist refugees from Tirol frequently stopped on the journey to Moravia. In 1534 Bastel Glaser, who was leading a company from Tirol to Auspitz in Moravia, was seized there with his party. It is to them that Hutter wrote this letter. The prisoners were later transferred from Hohenwart to Eggenburg where, perhaps at the same time, Peter Voit suffered his harsh imprisonment (see p. 16, footnote 1). At Eggenburg they had their cheeks burned through and were then released. Several songs written by Bastel Glaser are preserved in the Hutterian songbook. He was martyred in 1537. (M.E. II, p. 787; Wolkan, p. 105)

From the depth of our hearts we wish you the ineffable grace and mercy of God the heavenly Father, through our Lord Jesus Christ. Blessed be God the Father through Jesus Christ our Lord, who has made us worthy to suffer for the sake of His holy and almighty Name, who has called us out of the terrible darkness of this evil world and accepted us into the community of the chosen, who has given us citizenship in Heaven and unity with the hosts of angels. May God help us to reach the goal through His holy Name and through our Lord Jesus Christ.

Dearly beloved brothers and sisters! To our great sorrow we have understood that you are in prison, though it is for the sake of divine truth. But we have no idea how you are. Although we have sent brothers out to inquire, we have not heard anything about you.

We are very sad that we cannot speak to you or see you face to face; our hearts are truly suffering with you. We pray fervently and constantly to God; in fact, all the believers, the entire Church of God here at

Auspitz, does not cease to intercede for you. We remember you before God and reach out to you constantly in holy, brotherly love to comfort you with the comfort we ourselves have received from God. We ask you to remain steadfast in divine truth to the end through the love and mercy of God. Do not let the threats of the godless frighten you, for they cannot pluck one hair from your head unless it is God's will. Reverence God the Lord in your hearts, as the Apostle Peter says, which means, give honor to God and not to the godless; praise God, glorify Him, trust Him from the very depth of your hearts, and do not doubt His help. At times it may seem that He has abandoned you, but this will never happen. Though God sends you tribulation, He will also lead you out again. Do not forget the comfort of the Holy Spirit, which God has given all His children from the beginning through His prophets and servants.

2 Cor.
1:4

1 Pet.
3:14,15

1 Sam.
2:6,7
Tob.
13:2

This is what God says to His own: "Fear not, my servant, you poor wretched worm! I will be with you in fire and water." That is to say, "In all your tribulation, fear, and

Isa.
41:14;
43:2

need, I will be your King and Captain, yes,
your Watchman and Overseer." Therefore

Ps.
27:1-3

David proclaims, "The Lord is my shield
and weapon and my light—whom shall I
fear? The Lord is the refuge of my life—of
whom shall I be afraid? Though a whole
army should encamp against me, yet shall
my heart trust in the Lord!" Listen
carefully, dear brothers and sisters, to
what David testifies through the Holy

Ps.
3:6

Spirit! He cries, "I will not fear ten
thousands of people, and my heart shall
rely on the Lord alone, for with Him I
shall perform deeds and miracles." So do
the same, you dear ones.

Rom.
8:31

The Apostle Paul declares, "If God is
for us, who will be against us?" Christ

John
10:28,29

says, "No one will snatch out of my hand
those who are mine, for the Father who
has given them to me is stronger than all."

Isa.
40:17,23

And the Prophet Isaiah testifies, "All in
Heaven and on earth, nay, all kings and
princes, all men and creatures and all Gen-
tiles are as nothing compared with God."

What precious words these are for all
who love God—ponder them in your

Matt.
7:24,25

hearts! For Christ said, "He who hears my

words and diligently carries them out is like a wise and prudent man who builds his house on a rock; even though rain, wind, and water come and beat upon the house, it does not fall." The house represents all believing hearts in whom God dwells; the rock is Christ; the pelting rains and waters are the trials and persecutions and all the threats and suffering the world inflicts, and all false teachings. All these things cannot turn the believers away from the truth. Christ says: "On this rock will I build my holy Church, and the gates of Hell shall not overcome it." The gates of Hell represent the mighty ones of this world: kings, princes, tyrants, all the enemies of divine truth. In Paul's words, it is the princes of darkness and rulers of this world that we have to fight against.

Matt. 16:18

Eph. 6:12

Christ is the Gate leading to eternal life, and those who follow Him, who trust in Him wholeheartedly and obey Him, will be saved. The mighty ones are the gates leading to Hell and eternal death, and whoever believes and follows them will certainly be condemned. Yet they cannot turn God's children away from the truth, for Christ promised that the gates of Hell will not overcome the Church. The Apostle Peter says the same: "Who is there to harm you if you are zealous for what is right? Have no fear of their threats." If we actively bring forth fruits of the Holy Spirit in faith, we shall not come to grief.

1 Pet. 3:13,14

Paul the Apostle writes that "the hope we have in Christ Jesus will never disappoint us, for the love of God has been poured into our hearts." This love is Christ and the Father himself, in the words of John. It is also the Rock we must build on. Paul goes on to say,

Rom. 5:5

1 John 4:9

> Who shall separate us from the love of Christ? Shall tribulation, or distress, or persecution, or famine, or nakedness, or peril, or sword? As it is written, "For thy sake we are being killed all the day long; we are regarded as sheep to be slaughtered." No, in all these things we are more than conquerors through him who loved us. For I am sure that neither death, nor life, nor angels, nor principalities, nor things present, nor things to come, nor powers, nor

height, nor depth, nor anything else in all creation, will be able to separate us from the love of God in Christ Jesus our Lord.

(Rom. 8:35-39, RSV)

Dear children of God, see what powerful and comforting words these are! Paul also says, "The Lord is faithful and true and will not let you be tempted beyond your strength, but with the temptation the gracious Father will also provide a way for you to withstand it." When he says, "Have nothing to do with their idolatry," he means, keep clear of all their evil works; and whatever is laid upon you on that account, God will faithfully help you to bear it. He will aid you and stand by you in all your need. My beloved fellow members in the Body of Christ, see how wonderfully the Holy Spirit comforts us, whatever happens. When a lover of God ponders this and takes it into his heart, it makes his spirit leap and laugh for joy. If a man were sorrowful unto death, these words of comfort should fill him with new life, for all this and much more has been written down for our joy and consolation.

I Cor. 10:13

I Cor. 10:14

1 Sam.
2:6,7
Job
5:18

Be comforted then, for God leads into Hell and out again; He makes us sad and joyful again; He gives death and also life, and after great storms He makes the sun shine again. Therefore wait patiently for the redemption of your bodies, and do not grow faint or weary in the race. Do not look back either, but see to it that the love in your hearts does not grow cold and die. Do not be ashamed of the bonds and suffering of Christ; rejoice in them with your whole heart. You know that on this earth you are not promised anything but suffering and death, fear and need, and that the godless will persecute, torment, and dishonor you. This is the true sign of all God's faithful children; it is the sign of Christ, of the Son of Man and all His members. This sign will appear at the end-time too, according to the Word of the Lord; cross and tribulation are very fitting for all God's children. They are an honor in the sight of God the Most High and of all the believers, a glory and a garland of joy before Him. Christ the Lord had to suffer, and so did all the patriarchs and prophets and disciples, indeed, all the chosen from the beginning of the world.

If such things befall us for the sake of truth, we should remember what this means; we are not enemies of God but rather His friends and children. For the Lord himself says, "I discipline those whom I love." Every son whom the Father receives He chastises; He will not spoil him. But those who will not accept this discipline are not children of God but of the Babylonian harlot. It is written, "Happy are those who suffer the chastisement of the Lord." Throughout Scripture, those who stand the test and remain steadfast are called blessed by the Holy Spirit and given high praise before God. "Blessed are they who mourn, for they shall be comforted." This means those who for the Lord's sake bear sadness and grief and those who are persecuted for the sake of truth, for theirs is the Kingdom of Heaven. "Blessed are you when men revile you on my account; rejoice and be glad, for great is your reward in Heaven, for in the same way men persecuted the holy prophets before you." It is as if Christ were saying: By this you shall clearly recognize that you are made holy and are truly pleasing to

Prov
3:12
Rev.
3:19
Heb.
12:6

Job
5:17

Matt.
5:4

Matt.
5:11,12

God, for He has marked you with the
marks of those who love Him. Only of His
own does Christ say that they will be
crucified, persecuted, scourged, reviled,
robbed, banished, tormented, and put to
death. The Apostle Paul states that only
through much pain and tribulation can we
enter the Kingdom of God. If we are
fellow sufferers, we shall also be fellow
heirs; if we endure with Christ, we shall
also reign with Him. Paul writes, "It has
been granted to you not only to believe in
Christ but also to suffer with Him and to
fight the same fight which you have seen to
be mine." He simply wants to point men to
the Crucified Christ and to the Word that
speaks of suffering and the Cross. The
Apostle Peter has the same word: "If you
suffer and endure for doing right, you
have God's full approval." He says,
"Blessed are you if you suffer for
righteousness' sake, because God's Spirit
rests on you and is praised in you and
through you." James too says, "We call
blessed all those who have endured
chastisement."

There are many more wonderful

John
16:33
Matt.
10:17-22

Rom.
8:17

Phil.
1:29,30

1 Pet.
2:20

1 Pet.
4:14

James
5:11

testimonies telling us not to be ashamed of or shrink from the bonds and suffering of Christ, but to accept them from God with great thankfulness and joy. For this reason the apostles thanked God when they were tortured, reviled, and beaten with switches. Joyfully they went from the magistrates' presence, praising and thanking God from their hearts for being considered worthy to suffer shame and blows for the Lord's sake. They regarded it as something noble and precious. The Apostle Paul even boasted about the suffering and Cross of Christ that he endured in his own body. Peter also urges, "Let none of you suffer as an evildoer; yet if one of you suffers for being a Christian, he should not be ashamed but should praise and glorify God." And James pleads, "Count it all joy, my brethren, when you meet trials of every sort." Take comfort from these words, my beloved brothers and sisters, and remain valiant in the truth, for Christ says, "He who endures to the end will be saved." Fight loyally unto death for God's truth, and God will fight for you. Set no restrictions or time limits on the Lord's mercy;

2 Cor. 12:9,10

1 Pet. 4:15,16

James 1:2

Matt. 24:13

He knows the right hour; He will come at the right time, the very best time.

Matt.
10:32,33
Beloved ones, if you acknowledge the Lord faithfully, He will also acknowledge you in the presence of His heavenly Father. Be not ashamed of Him before this adulterous generation; then He will not be ashamed of you before God. If a man does not acknowledge Christ before all men, but denies Him and feels ashamed of Him, Christ will deny that man before God and all the angels. He will feel ashamed of him before all His heavenly hosts on that Day. But he who overcomes the Devil and his own flesh and all unrighteousness, who valiantly fights his way through this tem-

Wis.Sol.
5:16
1 Pet.
5:4
Rev.
2:10
poral death to life everlasting—on his head God the Lord will place a fair crown. He will receive from the Lord's hand an unfading garland.

Rev.
21:4
God will wipe away every tear from the eyes of the faithful and will grant them such inexpressible joy that they will never again think of the tribulations they had to suffer; these will be totally surpassed by

Rom.
8:18
glorious joy. In Paul's words, "I consider that the sufferings of this time are not

worth comparing with the glory that will
be revealed to us." He says, too, "Our suf- 2 Cor.
4:17
fering, which is slight and small, will bring
forth a glory that is great and splendid
beyond all measure." Both Paul and John
tell us that we shall be given a new, 1 John
3:2
heavenly nature and shall become like the
Lord, for we shall see Him as He is; our
bodies will be changed and become like Phil.
3:21
His own shining Body. Indeed, the elect 2 Esd.
7:97
will shine in their Father's Kingdom like Matt.
13:43
the beautiful, bright sun. What a glorious
Kingdom God has prepared and given to
His own, a Kingdom such as no eye has
ever seen, no ear has ever heard, and such
as never entered into a man's heart. We
know from the Prophet Esdras and the
Apostle Paul that the Lord will give eter- 2 Esd.
7:91-98
nal rest and peace to His own and no one Heb.
4:3,9
shall offend them anymore; they shall be
with God the Father and with Jesus Christ
the King; they shall sit at table in God's Matt.
8:11
Kingdom with Abraham, Isaac, and Jacob Luke
22:30
and with all the prophets and saints of
God; and they shall live with all the hosts
of Heaven for ever and ever.

Indeed, neither I nor any of the brothers

can tell of the unutterable joy that God will grant the elect. The saints and prophets foretell it throughout Scripture, but in my weakness I cannot possibly set it all down here. Those who understand this with their hearts will have to gird their loins to fight for this glory with zeal and joy, for a fight it will be. May God the Lord help you and all of us to gain the victory in this fight and win the prize through His Son Jesus Christ. Praise, thanks, and glory be given to Him who rules in sovereign majesty for ever and ever. Amen.

I Cor.
9:24

Now I want to let you know how things are with us here. The Lord is with us, although we suffer much. Yet that is right and good, and we praise and thank God for it with all our hearts. Apart from this need, we live in great and holy love, in the joy and unity of the Holy Spirit, while all the time expecting trials and persecution even greater than what we are suffering now.[1] May God watch over us through

---

[1]This severe persecution expected by Hutter did indeed break out in the following year, 1535. (Wolkan, pp. 108-110) See Letter IV.

His great mercy! With deep longing we
wait for the redemption of our bodies, for
the Sabbath when we rest from all trial ^{Heb.} Heb. 4:9,10
and labor and from all works of our own,
when we leave behind this earthly tent and 2 Cor. 5:4
when our soul and spirit may at last find
rest and eternal joy. For this divine 2 Esd. 7:91
homeland we yearn, since we have no
peace or rest in this wretched wilderness.
We have no permanent home here but are Heb. 13:14
awaiting one that is to come. Brother
Offrus has arrived, and many other
brothers and sisters.[1] We thank God for
protecting them and bringing them safely
to us. Their arrival gave us much joy, and
we praised God for it. There are not many
brothers and sisters left now in the mountains of Tirol.

Finally, the brothers Hans, Georg
Fasser, Offrus, Leonhart, Wilhelm, and all
the Servants of God here greet you,[2] and

[1]Wolkan, p. 106.

[2]Hans Amon had come from Tirol some time before Offrus
Griesinger. (Wolkan, p. 105) Leonhart Schmerbacher and
Wilhelm Griesbacher were both Servants of Temporal Need in
Auspitz and took an active part in Jakob Hutter's struggle with
Gabriel and Philipp in the fall of 1533. Wilhelm Griesbacher
suffered a martyr's death in 1535. (Wolkan, pp. 77-79; Beck, pp.
119-120)

so does the whole community, every one of God's children. We greet you a thousand times in holy love from the depths of our hearts and with the kiss of our Lord and Savior Jesus Christ. And I, Jakob, an unworthy servant of our Lord Jesus Christ and of His Church, greet you with all my heart a thousand times with the holy kiss of brotherly, Christian love.

I have written this to you with my own hand in the love of God. May my simple words challenge and hearten you. I would much rather speak with you face to face, but this is not possible now. So I commend you to God, to His gracious care and protection. May you be kept under His mighty arm and under the wings of His mercy. May He be with you forever, and may He gather us all into His peace through the Holy Spirit. May He bind us to each other and to Him in His truth and keep us firm as long as we live and in all Eternity, through our Lord Jesus Christ. To Him be praise, honor, and glory from our hearts for ever and ever. Amen.

LETTER IV

Letter IV, written on the open heath near Tracht
after the community was driven away from Auspitz
in 1535, is addressed to the Governor of Moravia,
Johann Kuna von Kunstadt. Different in style and
tone from any of the other letters, it appeals to the
Governor on behalf of the distressed brothers and
sisters and warns him of God's punishment.

We are brothers who love God and His
truth, we are witnesses of our Lord Jesus
Christ, and we have been driven out of
many countries for the sake of God's
Name. We arrived here in Moravia where
we have been living together under the
Lord Marshal through God's protection.
To God alone we give praise forever.

This letter is to let you know, dear Governor of Moravia, that we received the order delivered by your servants. We already answered you by word of mouth and now want to do it also in writing. This is our answer: We have left the world and all its wrong and godless ways. We believe in God the Almighty and in His Son, Jesus Christ, who will protect us from evil forevermore. We have given ourselves to God the Lord in order to live according to His divine will and keep His commandments in the way Jesus Christ showed us.

Because we serve Him, do His will, keep His commandments, and leave behind all sin and evil, we are persecuted and despised by the whole world and robbed of all our goods. The same was done to all the men of God, to the prophets, and to Christ himself. King Ferdinand in particular has put many of our innocent brothers and sisters to death. He has robbed us of our homes and all our goods and persecuted us terribly. But through God's grace we were able to move to this country and have lived here for a time, recently under the Lord Marshal. We have not troubled or harmed anyone and have lived faithfully in the fear of God; everybody will confirm this. But now even the Marshal has given us notice and forced us to leave our houses and property.

So we now find ourselves out in the wilderness, under the open sky on a desolate heath. This we accept patiently, praising God that He has made us worthy to suffer for His Name. Yet we feel great pain of heart for you, that you treat God's faithful children so cruelly. We cry to Him about your wretchedness. The enormous injustice increases daily. Day and night we plead with God the Lord to protect us from evil; we trust Him to lead us through, according to His will and mercy. And God will surely do so; He is our Captain and Protector and will fight for us. The Prophets Isaiah and Esdras foretold that 2 Esd. 16:74 all who turn away from evil, all who love Isa. 59:15 God from their hearts, who fear and serve Him and keep His commandments, are bound to be robbed and driven from their homes. This shows that we are fellow heirs Rom. 8:17 of His glory, that He loves us and is

pleased with us, and that we belong to the
believers. Therefore we quietly suffer all
this, and our hearts are comforted by His
Holy Spirit.

Heb.
12:2-11

But woe to all who persecute, expel, and
hate us without cause, simply because we
stand for God's truth! Their condemnation and punishment is approaching and
will overtake them terrifyingly, here and in
Eternity. According to His holy prophets,
God will call the persecutors most terribly
to account for the suffering and the innocent blood of His children.

Deut.
32:23-25,35,
41-43
Joel
3:1-8,19,20
Rev.
16:5-7

Now since you have commanded us to
leave without delay, we give you this
answer: We know of no place to go. We
are surrounded by the King's lands. In
every direction we would walk straight
into the jaws of robbers and tyrants, like
sheep cast among ravenous wolves.
Besides, we have among us many widows
and orphans, many sick people and
helpless little children who are unable to
walk or travel. Their fathers and mothers
were murdered by that tyrant Ferdinand,
an enemy of divine justice. He also robbed
them of their goods. These poor and weak

Matt.
10:16

ones are entrusted to us by God the Almighty, who commands us to feed, clothe, and house them, and in every way to serve them in love. So we cannot leave them behind or send them away—truly, may God protect us from ever doing that! We dare not disobey God for the sake of man's command, though it cost our life. We must obey God rather than men. ^{Acts 4:19}

We have not had time to sell our homes and possessions. They were earned by honest, hard labor, by the sweat of our brows, and rightly belong to us before God and men. We also need time because of the sick, the widows and orphans, and the small children. Praise God, there are not just few but many of these helpless ones among us, about as many as able-bodied people. Now, by God's will, we are out on the open heath, harming no one. We do not want to hurt or wrong anyone, not even our worst enemy, be it Ferdinand or anyone else. All our doing, our words and way of life, are there for all men to see. Rather than knowingly wrong a man to the value of a penny, we would let ourselves be robbed of a hundred florins;

rather than strike our worst enemy with
the hand—to say nothing of spears,
swords, and halberds as the world does—
we would let our own lives be taken.

As anyone can see, we have no physical
weapons, neither spears nor muskets. No,
we want to show by our word and deed
that men should live as true followers of
Christ, in peace and unity and in God's
truth and justice. We are not ashamed to
give an account of ourselves to anyone. It

Matt.
5:11,12
Luke
6:22,23
John
16:2-4
1 Pet.
4:4

does not trouble us that many evil things
are said about us, for Christ foretold all
this. It has been the lot of all believers, of
Christ himself, and of all His apostles,
from the beginning.

It is rumored that we took possession of
the field with so many thousands, as if we
were going to war, but only a callow, lying
scoundrel could talk like that. We lament
that there are so few believers (such as we
truly are). We wish all the world lived like
us; we would like to convince and turn all
men to this faith, for that would mean the
end of warfare and injustice.

In our present situation we just do not
know how we can leave the country unless

God the Lord in Heaven shows us where
to go. You cannot simply deny us a place
on the earth or in this country. For the
earth is the Lord's, and all that is in it
belongs to our God in Heaven. Besides,
even if we did agree to go, and planned to
do so, we might not be able to keep our
word, for we are in God's hands, and He
does with us whatever His will is. Perhaps
God wants us to remain in this country to
test our faith. This we do not know, but we
trust in the eternal and true God.

On the other hand, it is a fact that we
are being persecuted and driven out, so we
tell you that if the almighty God showed
us enough cause to leave the country and
move somewhere else, if He gave us good
proof that this were His will, we would do
it gladly, without waiting for any command from men. Once God's will about
where we should go is clear to us, we will
not hesitate. We will not and cannot disobey His divine will; neither can you, even
though you may think you can. God the
Almighty may suddenly reveal to us, even
overnight, that we should leave you. Then
we will not delay but be prepared to do

Ps.
24:1
I Cor.
10:26

His will—either to leave or to die. Perhaps you are not worthy to have us among you any longer.

Therefore woe to you Moravian lords forever, that you have given in to Ferdinand, the awful tyrant and enemy of divine truth, that you have agreed to drive those who love and fear God out of your lands. You fear a weak, mortal man more than the living, eternal, and almighty God. You are willing to expel and ruthlessly persecute the children of God, old and young, even the Lord's widows and orphans in their need and sorrow, and to deliver them up to plunder, fear, great suffering, and extreme poverty. It is as if you strangled them with your own hands. We would rather be murdered for the Lord's sake than witness such misery inflicted on innocent, God-fearing hearts. You will have to pay dearly for it and will have no more excuse than Pilate, who also did not want to crucify and kill the Lord Jesus. Yet when the Jews threatened him (by God's plan), fear of the Emperor made him condemn an innocent man. You do the same, using the King as your excuse.

John
19:4-7,12

God has made it known through the mouth of His prophets that He will avenge innocent blood with terrible might on all who stain their hands with it. Therefore you will earn great misfortune and distress, deep sorrow—indeed, eternal torment. They are ordained for you by God in Heaven, in this life and forever. In the name of our Lord Jesus Christ, we declare that this will certainly happen, and you will soon see that we have spoken the truth. This we declare to you and to all who sin against God.

Joel 3:1-3
2 Esd. 15:5-15, 21-27
Jude 15

We wish you could escape this judgment and that you and all men might be saved with us and inherit eternal life. For the sake of God we plead with you to accept His Word and our warning and to take them to heart, for we testify to what we know and to the truth of God. And we do this from a pure fear of God and because we love God and all men.

And now we entrust ourselves to the protection of the eternal Lord. May He be gracious to us and forever dwell with us, through Jesus Christ. Amen. As for you, may God the Lord allow you to understand His fatherly warning and discipline, and may He be merciful to you through our Lord Jesus Christ. His will be done. Amen.

LETTER V

In August 1535 Jakob Hutter was again in Tirol, where the Brotherhood had sent him for his own safety, unaware that this only intensified the danger. In both Moravia and Tirol the believers were under severe persecution; in Moravia the communities had been scattered. Four letters (V to VIII) are preserved from this time, all written from Tirol to Moravia in the year 1535.

Letter V, the first one of these, was carried by a brother called Michel. Here Jakob Hutter insists on the need to hold firmly to the truth he had taught the brothers and sisters. He would spare them their suffering by taking it on himself, if that were possible.

From Jakob, unworthy servant of God and apostle of Jesus Christ and His Church, His holy Bride purified by His own blood:

Grace, peace, and everlasting mercy to all the believers. This I wish from the bottom of my heart for all my beloved brothers and sisters in the Lord and in the faith, for my longed-for and obedient children in Moravia, who are pursued and scattered and who suffer distress and poverty for the sake of the Lord. May God our heavenly Father, who is the gracious and merciful Comforter, console and strengthen you and stand by you with His help in all your troubles, through Jesus Christ. Amen.

You faithful children of the living God, those whom He has chosen and sanctified, my fellow members in the Body of Jesus Christ, what mighty things has God done for us! He has shown us inexpressible mercy. We shall never praise and glorify Him enough, never thank Him enough! Through His Son Jesus Christ He redeems us from everlasting death and grants us eternal life if we remain faithful on the way of Christ to the end.

My dear children, how great is the love of the Heavenly Father for you because you love Him and keep His commandments, obey His holy will, and follow the footsteps of Christ, living according to His words! The heavenly hosts rejoice over you and constantly praise God because He has pleasure in you. The Father showed His immeasurable love and grace by sending to this earth His beloved Son Jesus Christ, who suffered death for you. Through the Son you have become dear to God, His chosen children, witnesses to His eternal truth and fellow heirs of His might and glory. You share His divine nature, you are citizens of Heaven, and you have fellowship with God and all who dwell in the heavenly Jerusalem. He has become your merciful Father and your best friend. From Him you may expect every good thing that His fatherly love can give.

His almighty Name be blessed and exalted in Heaven above, where He is enthroned in glory. My heart is filled with thanks to God for the unfathomable grace and mercy He continually shows to you, to us, and to all believers.

Because you have forsaken the world and become followers of Christ and because you love God, God also loves you; and for the very reason that God loves you, the world hates you, and all godless

men will persecute and revile you. But
rejoice, for they did the same to all the
prophets and to the Lord himself and to
all the chosen from the beginning. It is a
clear sign and seal of God's favor.

You dear brothers and sisters know that
through the grace of the Lord I have
served Him and you in my weakness for
quite some time here in Tirol, as I did
among you in Moravia.[1] I have done this
faithfully day and night without any
falsehood or deceit, out of sincere
brotherly love, and I have suffered much
pain and heartache from the many
tribulations that have come upon me. In
spite of these trials I have cared for you as
a devoted father cares for his children,
whom he loves with his whole heart. This I
can truthfully boast about before God. I
trust the Father that I will never be made
ashamed of my boasting, for I do it only to
glorify the Lord. He dwells in me and
stands by me in all of my many
weaknesses; of that I boast.

2 Cor.
10:8

[1] Hutter was in Moravia (Auspitz) from August 1533 until July
1535. At Whitsun 1535 he married Katharina Purst. In August
he returned with his wife to Tirol, where this letter was written.
(Fischer, p. 38)

You know, beloved ones, that God very soon allowed terrible persecution to come upon me and all of us. Therefore with earnest pleading to the Lord you urged me to take leave of you. You sent me forth in a way pleasing to God, as your beloved brother, your Servant and Shepherd given by His grace. I know I am quite unworthy of so much respect and so much heartfelt brotherly love as you have shown me. May God in Heaven reward you for this love and faithfulness to me and to all the believers. May He repay you here and in His eternal Kingdom, through Jesus Christ. Truly, you dear ones chosen by the Lord, my soul does not cease praising God for the great love He has given into your hearts. O beloved brothers and sisters, I cannot find words to express it well, but may it be God alone who is glorified in all this, and may our hearts honor and thank Him through Jesus Christ for ever and ever. Amen.

So I left you at your request, obeying the decision you arrived at by God's leading. You know this caused my heart great sorrow even though it was according

to the will of the living God in Heaven.
Yes, I left you with weeping and many a
deep sigh, and the pain is still in my heart
and will remain unless God sends
comfort—and that He will surely do. May
the Lord give me and all of us patience to
wait for His comfort and the fulfillment of
His promise. And He has comforted me
already so that the grief would not be too

I Cor.
10:13

great for me. God is faithful and will not
let us be tried beyond what we can bear;
when temptation comes He provides a way
out at the same time so that we can endure
it, as the Apostle Paul writes. These words
are really true; I have experienced it many

Rom.
5:4

times. Experience makes a man grow in
wisdom and in understanding of God's
ways and teaches him to have hope and
childlike trust in God.

Now, brothers and sisters, I want to let
you know how we are. After we parted
from you, God the Lord of the heavenly
Kingdom protected our journey and
speeded our way to the Puster and Adige
valleys. Here we found our brothers and
sisters and greeted each other in God's

love. We were welcomed with great joy.
We reported to them how everything is
going, and they reported to us. Since then
we have been traveling in the mountains
and valleys, seeking out those who hunger
and thirst for the truth. We found many
who received us with joy and gratitude and
with eager hearts, and we taught them
from the Word of God, the holy Gospel.
Several accepted the truth and gave their
lives to God.

So the Almighty Father has again
established His Church here in Tirol and
multiplies His people daily, adding to the Acts
2:47
Church those who are being saved. We
have very much work to do for the Lord,
day and night. As soon as we arrive at one
place, we wish we could be at many other
places at the same time. We need more
Servants of the Word and other brothers
fitted for the task and able and willing to
carry out God's work.[1] The harvest is ripe, Matt.
9:37
but the workers are few.

[1]Servants of the Word were chosen by the members to teach and
guide the Church according to the Gospel. They were often sent
on dangerous mission journeys, facing the possibility of
imprisonment, torture, and death.

The decision that I should come here was not made in vain or without good reason; it did not come from men, from the flesh, but from God, and it was very necessary. But when I say more of us are needed here, I do not mean that everybody should now take it upon himself to come running without the permission and knowledge of the Servants and of the whole Church. We will not receive anyone who comes like this, and God will also punish him from Heaven. But whoever is sent by God and His Church, whoever comes in love, in the fear of God and in the truth, we will receive with joy and thankfulness, in brotherly love, as we would receive the Lord himself.

Gal.
4:14

It seems that the authorities, who are enemies of the truth and have the power to kill, do not yet know that we are here. May God in Heaven keep them blind and unaware of it for a long time.

It is not for my own sake that I wish this, as if I feared for my life; I thank God for taking all my fear away. In Him I trust that fear cannot overcome me. I would willingly lose my life for the sake of His people. I have completely surrendered and sacrificed my body to the Lord; with all my heart I am willing to suffer and die for His sake, for His truth. I will do whatever He lays upon me, in the way that honors Him the most and is the best help to His children for the building-up of His Church. It is for the sake of those who are young and not yet firm in faith that I hope our lives are spared until God's fire has been so brightly kindled in them and His work so well established that even great floods and torrents of rain will not be able to quench the fire. I pray for this according to the Father's will, and ask you, my dear fellow members, to do the same if you want to show us true love. I do not doubt your heartfelt love for us. I know you well, as a devoted shepherd knows his sheep, and I am sure that you also know me.

Severe persecution is bound to break out before too long, or even right away, unless God himself delays it for His name's sake and for the sake of His people. The enemies of the truth are growing fierce and bloodthirsty toward the believers. There is a great hue and cry all over the country

and everyone talks about you and us, how
we have been persecuted and driven out.
They spread all kinds of stories, as they
usually do.

I know that you dear ones have been
longing for some news of us, and it is long
overdue. I have had in mind the whole
time that I promised to send you word as
soon as possible, as soon as God enabled
me. He knows that I have not forgotten
you for a single hour. This is the reason for
the delay: brother Jeronimus does not
know this area, and for a long time we
were not able to reach brother Kränzler,
for he was ill at Sterzing.[1] He also does not
know all the roads in the Puster Valley, or
the people who are seeking God. So we
turned to the most urgent task, making
visits all over the place in order to
acquaint the other brothers with the roads

[1] Jeronimus Käls was a much loved schoolmaster of the Church
in Moravia. He wrote teachings and prayers for the children.
(M.E. III, pp. 139-140; Wolkan, pp. 119-123) In Tirol he was
one of Jakob Hutter's co-workers in the mission task. He suffered martyrdom and death for his faith.

Brother Kränzler is mentioned again at the end of Letter VII
as one of those sending special greetings. All we know otherwise
is that he was executed in 1536, the same year as Jakob Hutter.
(Beck, p. 131)

and villages, and at the same time we did some work for the Lord. That is why I could not spare brother Michel. Actually I still need him very badly, but because of my love for you I did not keep him any longer but hurried him on his way to bring you our comfort. I have great hope that the Lord will send me more help through you. I hope you will understand this and accept it from me in the love of God.

Beloved brothers and fellow members, I have been waiting and longing for a message from you too. I am still waiting, and my heart has no rest, day or night. My soul and spirit long for you, I yearn and sigh for you. You are the true, living letter written in my heart, not with pen and ink but by God's finger—that is, by His Word and Spirit and His burning love. This letter is with us all the time. *2 Cor. 3:2,3*

O my dearest children, what constant pain and sorrow I bear for you! I think of you day and night, yes, the whole time, and I sigh often and shed many hot tears in my distress for you. Not that you have given me reason to be ashamed of you but because of my deep love for you. I am like

a devoted father thinking of his children
who are far away and in misery; not knowing how they are, he fears for them. So it is
with me. God knows I am not lying; He is
my witness that I speak the truth.

How often my eyes and my heart
overflow! I pour out my grief to God and
will go on crying to Him until He comforts
me. My distress and pain have been great
since I heard that you are being scattered.
O God in Heaven, I cannot cry enough to
Thee! For with God's help I would suffer
great persecution, pain, and torture if only
you brothers and sisters could remain
together in love. I am speaking of those
who long with all their hearts to remain
together through God's love and Spirit. It
is not only the physical separation that
worries me, but the greater and everlasting
harm it could bring to the souls of many.
May God protect the believers from it.

My most beloved brothers and sisters,
my little lambs, how I long to find you
again! I labored long and hard in love to
gather you. I also suffered for you. And
now the ravening wolves come to scatter,
to crush with their claws, and what is left

Dan.
7:7

they trample underfoot, as the prophet
Daniel says. What shall I say? It makes my
heart break. O God, have pity!

My dear children, I can hardly write, my
sorrow is so great. But that is not because
my conscience accuses me of causing the
scattering—no, I am not guilty of it. (I
myself have had a hard life, my God
knows that.) It is an abomination and a
heartache to me, and I have always
faithfully warned of it and fought against
it. But the Lord allows those godless
enemies of truth to persecute and scatter
us, and I can do no more than endure it
with patience and sorrow. So no one
should think I am to blame. My heart is
free of guilt. I am innocent of all blood. It
is the brood of the Devil—like ravening Ezek.
wolves, as Scripture says—who have done 22:23-27
this. My helpers and I have faithfully
gathered you and held you together.

Through God's grace and Spirit I
foretold all this. Did I not warn you constantly for two years of what has now
happened? How strongly and clearly was
this said so that you would expect it and
live accordingly. I pleaded with you to

listen to God's Word, to take it into your
hearts, and to keep it there faithfully so
that you could turn to it in times of need.
God may yet cause His Word to become
scarce among you and take us from you or
you from us, in whatever way He wills. I
told you all this, and I encouraged you to
hold on to faith even if we are separated. I
challenged you to trust in God, to serve
and confess Him, and to have Him always
before your eyes, to fear and love Him
from your hearts, and to love one another
as His faithful children. I challenged you
to be eager always to do God's will, keep
His commandments, and endure in His
truth to the end so that you may be blessed
and rejoice with us eternally. I taught you
how to live before God and all the
brothers and sisters and all men.

And already the hour has come. Happy
are they who listened carefully to God's
Word, who kept it in their hearts, and who
now live and walk faithfully! My beloved
brothers and sisters, if only I could ward
off your suffering with my own body. How
willingly would I present my cheek, my
back, and all my members to the torturers

and surrender my body to any torment, with the help of God! But why say this? We cannot change anything. May God himself be our Shepherd and Watchman so that none are snatched out of His hand and lost. The hour of trial has truly come. May God give us patience to be steadfast in our hope for comfort and joy.

I feel as the Prophet Jeremiah did: O you holy City of the Most High, how shall I mourn you! You holy garden of the Lord, what great joy and delight I have often had in you! How many beautiful and fragrant flowers bloomed in you and gave great joy to the Lord! O people of God, heavenly and eternal Jerusalem, happy the man who speaks well of you and wishes you well, but woe to all those who speak evil of you, who persecute and destroy you! The Lord will requite them for their deeds. Those who grieve for you and suffer with you will also rejoice with you, as God says through His prophets and apostles. This promise gladdens my heart, for I faithfully mourn and suffer with you and so hope to share your comfort too. I am certain before God and in Jesus Christ

Isa.
58:11
Jer.
31:12
Hos.
14:5-7

Isa.
61:3

that I must not and cannot ever forsake you. You dearly beloved ones, I can truly say with David: If I forget you, let God also forget me; I would rather forget my right hand or my soul than forget you.

Ps. 137:5,6

My dear children, may it be God's will that we still see one another on this earth in joy and godly love. O that the almighty and merciful Father might still gather us! How I long with my whole heart, soul, and spirit for this! How glad I would be on that day! Even if I had to suffer greatly for it, I still wish it for your sake. For my own sake I do not want to live. I would much rather be with my heavenly Father and with the throng of those who rejoice, who are at rest from all labor and freed from tribulation and care.

Ps. 42:4

But my dear children, I could not prevent what has happened, nor can I change the situation we are in now, though it breaks my heart. How gladly I would offer my life or endure terrible torture if only I could change your lot! If only I could bear all the pain for you myself! I know, of course, that my weeping is of no help, but Christ's love urges me and I cannot stop.

This same love urges me to plead with you, my children, to live completely according to the will of God and to follow the example and teaching of Jesus. I have taught you what is right before God. You must not doubt this way, for it is the truth, and you have heard us speak of it many times in the past, through God's Spirit. The truth has been clearly shown to you and I hope also to testify to it and give my blood for it, with God's help.

Love God with all your hearts and keep His commandments; then you will find blessedness. Eagerly do His will in whatever you may be doing, so that in the midst of this godless generation you will be a credit to the Lord and His holy ones. Shine like a light in the darkness. Let love flow among you from pure and undivided hearts, you who are like children, newborn from God's Word and Spirit. Serve each other faithfully and lovingly, each with the gifts God has given him, and do it gladly, without any murmuring or reluctance. For God loves and helps only those who joyfully do what is right, who serve Him and His people in the love of the Holy Spirit.

Whoever freely obeys and serves God the Lord with his whole heart, pleases God as His own dear child. So you must never tire of doing good or weaken in your determination. Do not allow laziness or sleepiness to creep into your discipleship. See to it that your love to God and His children, the true light of God in your heart, is not extinguished. You must never look back or long for what you left behind but always press on toward your goal. Then you will win the prize and receive the crown. Show willingness and respect to one another, and seek to be loving, brotherly, and warmhearted, as children of God should be. Patiently accept every trial, for you are disciples and lambs of Christ, and watch for God day and night. Faithfully follow the teachings of the apostles, which you have heard, and live in the unity of Jesus Christ with all the believers. Continue in the breaking of bread, which points to the life and love of Jesus Christ that should be among us. Pray to God night and day, in spirit and in

Phil.
3:13,14

John
4:24

truth, and believe firmly in our gracious Father.

Wake up, you faithful Christians, and lift your hearts up to God our heavenly Father! Let your joy be in Him and in His holy Law, and have your mind and spirit and your whole heart always turned to Heaven. Await your Bridegroom with pure hearts, in holy expectation and fear of God. He, your King and Redeemer, the Prince of Life and the true Shepherd, is coming and is not far off. He is Jesus Christ, our beloved Lord and Master. Put on the wedding garment, the holy robe of love, faith, hope, righteousness, and truth—yes, put on the Lord Jesus Christ, the Son of God. Arm yourselves with the good works of faith and with pure and God-fearing hearts so that you are found worthy of entering His joy and glory with Him.

Rom. 13:14
Gal. 3:27

O you whom I love most dearly, wake up, wake up for the Lord's sake, for your King is coming with great power! Time is running out, the hour has come. The great and terrible Day of the Lord, which will come upon all people, is near at hand. The

Matt.24 signs and wonders by which we are to
recognize it are here. They are present
everywhere, for every kind of sin, every
kind of evil, is taking over. Love has
grown cold in many. Everywhere the
Gospel is being proclaimed, and the sound
of it has gone through the whole world.
Many false prophets and antichrists have
arisen, and much innocent blood is shed.
The godless yield to unbridled godlessness;
their villainy has no bounds. As the holy
Dan. prophets say, the abomination of desola-
11:31;
12:11 tion reigns, and we behold all its violence
Matt.
24:15 and sin. Yes, everything the prophets and
Christ himself spoke of is rampant now.

It is also a fact that many people say,
Ezek. "Time passes and every vision comes to
12:22
nothing." And as the days pass, many
2 Pet. scoffers say, "Where is the promise of His
3:3,4
coming? Everything is the same as it has
always been." That is what Ezekiel and the
Apostle Peter foretold. These scoffers
deliberately refuse to listen.

What I fear most is that we will begin to
Matt. say, as many people do, "Oh, my Lord will
24:47-50
not come for a long time." And they eat
and drink and associate with the godless,

and they beat and torment their fellow servants, as Christ says in the parable. But the Lord will come on a day and at an hour when they are not expecting or thinking about Him. Just when they think everything is peaceful and as safe as can be, destruction will suddenly come upon them. God grant that this does not happen to any of us. It is not for nothing that the Lord said He will come like a thief in the night, when everybody is fast asleep and without a care in the world. *Matt. 24:43 Luke 12:39,40*

There are good reasons to fear that many followers of the Lord will be found asleep and unprepared at Christ's coming. He Himself warns us: "Be ready all the time. Watch constantly, every hour of the day and night, for you do not know the day or the hour when your Lord and King will come. He will come when you do not expect Him." Therefore watch and be ready every moment so that you are found worthy to enter with Him. Each one must hold firmly to the Lord and His Word until he is taken home, so that he is found pure before God. *Mark 13:32-37*

So accept trouble and suffering and

bear them patiently; embrace the Cross with great thankfulness to God, for it is holy and glorious. If you accept it in this way, it becomes a noble gift, showing God's love and mercy. For Christ says,

Matt.
5:10

"Blessed are all who bear suffering for my sake and are persecuted for the sake of divine truth and justice. They shall be comforted. The Kingdom of Heaven is

Isa.
35:10;
61:7
Jer.
31:13
John
16:20
Isa.
66:10

theirs." He also says, "Be comforted, my children, for your misery and sorrow shall turn into joy and great glory." Isaiah says, "Rejoice and break forth into singing, all you who mourn for Jerusalem, for you will also rejoice with her."

Ps.126

The patriarch David says, "When the Lord ends our captivity, we shall be full of joy and our mouths will be full of laughter and our hearts and tongues full of praise to God. We shall sow with tears but shall reap with gladness." Here we weep and are full of sorrow as we bear the precious seed, but then with great joy shall we bring our fruits of righteousness before God's countenance and receive the new fruit, the reward of eternal life and of the new Jerusalem. As Scripture says, distress and

sorrow precede glory, honor, and joy. The
Apostle Paul writes, "If we suffer with
Him, we shall be fellow heirs with Him; if
we endure with Him, we shall reign with
Him," and again, "Our suffering bears no
comparison with the joy and glory that
will be revealed to us." In another place he
says, "Our suffering, which is temporary
and slight, will bring us all-surpassing
splendor and joy." Peter also says, "If we
remain steadfast in all kinds of trials, have
faith in the Lord, and obey His Word,
then we will also exult with Him in inexpressible glory."

So rejoice and be comforted, you who
are faithful in Christ, for the reward God
will give is great and not far off. How very
much the prophets and all the believers
have said about this! You must cling to
God and His truth, to His holy Church
and Covenant. Fight courageously in
every trial, even to death; witness to God
in word and deed before this godless
generation; and serve God and His
children faithfully in obedience and with a
glad heart. So you must overcome the
whole world, the Devil, sin, and death,

Rom.
8:17

Rom.
8:18

2 Cor.
4:17

1 Pet.
4:13

and your own selves, striving manfully to fight your way from this evil world into the coming one and through this temporal death to eternal life.

Then God will set upon your head an unfading garland of glory. He will give you a kingdom that never ends. There you will have rest, great joy, and glory, which will never be taken from you. God will transfigure your body to be like the glorified body of Jesus Christ. He shines more brightly than the sun, and you too will shine like that in God's Kingdom. God will dress you in fine white garments and adorn you with precious jewels.

The Lord will descend from His Throne of glory with hosts of angels. He will awaken and gather His own with a mighty trumpet blast. In truth He is already doing it now, through the Spirit. He will take you and all the chosen to Himself with the multitude of His angels, and will lead you into His heavenly Kingdom. There we shall reign with the Lord for ever and ever and live in the sight of God with all the heavenly hosts and all believers. There will be unspeakable joy for ever and ever.

2 Esd. 2:43,46
1 Cor. 9:25
1 Pet. 5:4
Rev. 2:10
2 Esd. 7,90, 91,98
Phil. 3:21
2 Esd. 7:97
Matt. 13:43
Rev. 3:5; 6:11; 21:2
Matt. 24:30,31
1 Thess. 4:16,17
2 Tim. 2:12
Rev. 22:5

May the almighty and merciful God, Father of the heavenly Kingdom, help us all to enter there, through His Son Jesus Christ, our beloved Lord. Praise, honor, and thanks be to Him who is on High, on the Throne of glory, for ever and ever. Amen.

For the sake of the Lord I ask you, plead to God for us day and night. We depend on it, and we will do the same for you. We know God will hear your prayers. Of course we know that you already pray for us, but we urge you to continue and not slacken but rather to increase your petitions as time goes on.

Our dear Nändl is still in prison. Though she is allowed to walk about the place, they will not let her go. We hope that the Lord will set her free very soon. We will do all we can to help, if it is God's will.[1] She is faithful to the Lord and fears Him. She has a deep love for God and for all believers. We praise and honor God in Heaven, for she has found favor in His eyes. May she and we all be kept constant

[1] In Letter VII (p. 127) Jakob Hutter mentions that Nändl was released.

in His truth until the end. We sent a sister
to see Nändl, who greets you all warmly in
faithful and pure love with the holy kiss of
Christ. Her heart is on fire with love for
you. The same is true of the beloved
brothers and sisters here, the whole
Church of God, one and all.

Isa.
41:14

And I, Jakob, greet you. I am a miserable worm, yet a servant of the Lord
through His grace, your apostle and
shepherd; and I hope to be a brother to

Rev.
1:9

you, your companion in the suffering and
patient endurance of Jesus Christ and His
children. From the bottom of my heart I
greet you, all together and each one
individually, all of you who fear God and
love His children. I greet each one with the
holy kiss of our Lord Jesus Christ, in true
brotherly love, and I wish you the lasting
peace Christ has won for us. This I wish
for you constantly, and greet you with
heart, soul, and spirit. Before God and
men I think and speak nothing but good of
you, and I remember you in love, for truly
I love you with my whole heart. How I
wish I could greet each one of you personally with a holy kiss. I long to be with

you in body, soul, and spirit. May the Lord in Heaven, our beloved Father, dwell in you through Jesus Christ for ever and ever. Amen.

LETTER VI

Letter VI, from Tirol to Moravia in 1535, was written under the impact of growing persecution in both areas. Members who became unfaithful under this pressure betrayed their brothers and sisters. Suffering sifted out many who were halfhearted, and yet it stimulated new growth of the Brotherhood. More workers were needed to gather in the harvest.

Our sources report that this letter, as well as the following one, was carried by brother Christel Schmidt (also called Wölfl Zimmermann).

Jakob, an unworthy laborer of the Lord Jesus Christ, writing to the children of God in Moravia, who are expelled and scattered in all directions for their witness to God and for the sake of His holy Name. My beloved in the Lord, may the grace, the peace, and the everlasting mercy of our Heavenly Father be with you, and may He bless you through Jesus Christ. Amen.

Dearly beloved children of God, wherever you may be in Moravia,

persecuted for the sake of divine truth and
justice, I constantly thank and praise God
for you. All of us who are here, the
brothers and sisters in the Body of Jesus
Christ, pray for you earnestly all the time.
We are very much aware of your suffering
and poverty, beloved brothers and sisters,
and our hearts are very pained for you.
God in Heaven knows that all of us bear
this with you, that we suffer with you and
fear for you. But may our merciful Father,
who is the righteous Judge of all widows
and orphans and the Comforter of all suffering Christian souls, stand by us all in
our troubles. May He protect us and
deliver us from all tribulation. May He
graciously show us the way through and
comfort and cheer us in our misery. Let us
give all honor to our God in Heaven, the
Creator and Father full of mercy, for all
the children of God through Jesus Christ.

Most dearly beloved brothers and
sisters, not long ago I sent our brother
Michel to you. When I took leave of him, I
begged God to lead him safely and quickly
to you so that he could comfort you in

Luke
18:2-8

your misery. We have also prayed to God the Almighty that we might hear something from you. We have been eagerly waiting for news. With brother Michel I sent you a written report of everything that has happened here, to let you know how we are.[1] We trust God, our loving Father, that His angel led brother Michel to you and that you received our message.

I want to tell you briefly what has happened since then, to bring you up to date, as God's Spirit urges me. No sooner had we said good-bye to brother Michel than a brother arrived, bringing news of you. We welcomed him joyfully and gratefully as a beloved brother sent to us by God and by you, and what you wrote comforted us greatly.

We have read your letter over and over and thought much about what you wrote, about your steadfastness, your great patience and obedience on Christ's way, and your uprightness and courage. We rejoice in the manly fight of the martyrs

---

[1]This is a reference to Letter V, which was carried to Moravia shortly before by brother Michel.

and witnesses of God among you, who remained faithful even under torture and confessed valiantly to the Lord and His truth to the end.

We cannot thank and honor the Lord enough for all these witnesses. Glory be to His Name. Yes, we and many other faithful souls have been comforted and strengthened and given new trust in the Lord through your reports. How deeply we long with all our hearts to do as they have done. They are an inspiration and an example to us. May God grant us this through His beloved Son Jesus Christ, to His honor and glory.

At the same time we are deeply pained to hear how much evil and opposition has been spreading, and that many who had given themselves to God and were our brothers and sisters have lost the way because of this persecution and because they have given in to the temptations of the world. In a godless way they have broken their covenant with the Lord and His people. They go back on their promises and join the Devil and the world again, becoming enemies of God and His children. Alas for those people—what a severe sentence they will receive from God, what heavy punishment! It would be better for them if they had never known the truth, although in that case they would also fall under God's judgment.

We have been told of several who have lost the way and are excluded. With God's help this will not weaken us or harm us, for we know that those whose hearts are lukewarm must be separated from the faithful as chaff is separated from wheat by the wind and dross from silver and gold by fire. They will be sifted out in suffering and persecution, through false prophecy and through Satan's cunning and deceit. The Scriptures clearly foretell that many will turn away from the Cross of Jesus Christ. Led astray by false prophets, many will fall away from God and forsake and hate His righteousness and His holy people. This happened already at the time of the prophets, and at the time of Christ and His apostles. So it should not discourage us or separate us from the love of God.

Since men of God have warned us that this would happen and we are well aware

Malachi 3:3
Matt. 3:12
Luke 22:31
Isa. 30:1
Jer. 5:23
Luke 8:13
Heb. 6:6

of it, now let us turn our eyes all the more to the steadfast and obedient children of God, those who have been faithful till death, though they are few in our time. And let us pay no attention to the rebellious and unfaithful, however great their number.

A man who is upright before God, who lives in the truth and fights for it till the end, who witnesses to the Lord under torture and in every temptation remains true to God and His people—that man is worth more in God's eyes than a hundred thousand unbelievers and unfaithful men. And he should also be precious to our hearts. Let us learn from such a man and follow his example. Let us abide in the Lord with those who belong to Him, those in whom God's Spirit dwells and who bear the living Word and the Name of God in their hearts. Some of those who have gone astray and are no longer faithful to the Lord, who are now revealed as false and have been excluded by you, had already caused me concern earlier. May God protect us from following their example and falling into the snare the Devil has

I Pet.
1:22,23

caught them in. Let us pray that these things do not continue to happen and that we are not found unfaithful. O God in Heaven, protect those who fear and seek Thee!

Beloved brothers and sisters, we must be therefore all the more God-fearing and faithful and guard carefully against the sins that cling to us and our natural weaknesses. As the Apostle Paul says, we must no longer let sin rule our mortal bodies, no longer give in to sin and the Devil; we must not let our limbs be used as tools of injustice or sin. Instead let us love God and have Him and His children always before our eyes. Let us be obedient to the Lord and His people, ready and eager to do His work. We are determined to do this, but God our merciful Father must accomplish it in us to glorify His holy Name through His Son Jesus Christ.

Rom. 6:12

Phil. 2:12,13

To know of your great suffering, your misery and poverty, gives us another reason to feel pain and compassion for you. We suffer with you because we love you. The hearts of all brothers and sisters here are deeply distressed and filled with sorrow. My own grief will not be stilled, as I wrote to you before. My heart weeps and mourns for you day after day. God in Heaven, who knows me, is my witness; He knows the thoughts of all human hearts; every secret is laid bare to Him. So in deep sorrow, with an anxious heart and eyes wet with tears, I write to you again, my beloved children in the Lord. May God comfort all of us in His Son Jesus Christ, through the great compassion of His heart, and with the Holy Spirit! May He help us and stand by us in our misery. We entrust ourselves to Him in this life and in Eternity. Amen.

Heb.
4:12,13

Dear brothers and sisters, let the living truth be your comfort and strength. It is being proclaimed to you now and you have heard it before. Do not waver or lose courage, for this is the right way, the truth witnessed to by Scripture. Many in this country and in other lands have shed their blood for it and left this world. You are the chosen race and royal priesthood, a holy nation, God's own people. You are the Church of the Firstborn, whose names

1 Pet.
2:9

Heb.
12:23

are written in Heaven; and you are fellow workers and children of the living God. God's heart delights in you as a father delights in his beloved children, which He is constantly proving to you. So you should not doubt His favor, for He has sealed it among you in Moravia through the agony endured by your faithful fighters for the truth. They witnessed to it with their blood, giving great honor to the Lord. They are like a wonderful garland of joy for us, a comfort and strengthening from God.

1 John 3:1

1 Thess. 2:19

Though many condemn you and us, do not be alarmed, for their slander and reviling cannot hurt us as long as God our Father is with us and is pleased with us! So take courage. God looks upon us with grace and compassion. To Him who sits upon the Throne of Majesty be glory, honor, and thanks through Jesus Christ His beloved Son, from us and all the faithful and the heavenly hosts forever. Amen.

Dear children of God, in my love for you I want to write about the Church here.

Hos.
14:5-7

The brothers and sisters are growing in godly righteousness and flourishing like lovely tulips and sweet-scented lilies. As a garden bursts into leaf and flower after rain in May, so they are budding and blossoming in God's sight, flourishing in the fear of God and in His love and peace. Their hearts burn with God's pure love and are constantly kindled by His light and fire; I cannot praise and thank Him enough for this. I truly rejoice before God; my heart leaps for joy when I think of their obedience and the love and faithfulness God has given them. How richly the Almighty has blessed them! And even though they have all just started on God's way and have heard very little of His Word, still they have made a good and wholehearted beginning. May God help them to reach the end. They are a joy to my heart and deserve the name "garden of the Lord," as Scripture says. For them I praise and thank God with all my heart.

Ps.
92:12-14
Isa.
27:6

Isa.
58:11
Jer.
31:12

It is my heartfelt request to God that He will water His garden with rain from Heaven, with the comfort of His Holy Spirit and the oil of His compassion. May

Isa.
27:2,3;
45:8
Jer.
5:24

He anoint all our hearts, pouring heavenly blessing upon His garden, so that it is fruitful and bears many good works. This garden is the Church of the living God. He raised a fence around His garden to guard it from wild beasts; may He also protect it from bad thunderstorms and from evil blights so that the fruit may ripen, for the Lord's Eden is now in full bloom. May He himself keep watch over it and bring it to a bountiful harvest.

Song of Sol. 4:16
Hos. 14:5
Isa. 27:6;
45:8
Hos. 14:7
Song of Sol. 4:12

Isa. 27:3

You should know that our being here is no longer a secret; godless people know it and are very hostile, raising a great hue and cry. The clergy, those messengers of destruction, are already raging about us from their pulpits, warning people that we are in the country and up in the mountains and ordering them to attend their sacraments and worship their idols.[1] But the City built on the holy mountain of

Matt. 5:14

[1] The clergy took an active part in the persecution of the Anabaptists. As well as denouncing the Anabaptists from their pulpits, they took part in the efforts to make them recant, sometimes interrogating them day and night. This probably accounts for the strong language used by Jakob Hutter against Pope and clergy. We have felt it better, however, not to translate it in all its force.

Luke
8:16

John
1:5

Matt.
10:26
Luke
8:17

Isa.
57:20

Jon.
2:2

Zion cannot be hidden. The light shines out and is not covered up but burns brightly, like a lamp lighting up the darkness. This light is the children of God, for God kindled His flame in them. About this, Jesus says that there is nothing hidden that will not be revealed.

They threaten us with their judges, bailiffs, and executioners. So the sea of the wicked is roaring and raging. And I am afraid it will not rest until Jonah is cast in and the terrible whale has swallowed him. This Leviathan is King Ferdinand, the cruel tyrant and enemy of divine truth, with all his followers, and the misguided Pope with his accomplices. But God will command the sea to give back His own; like Jonah they will be delivered from the belly of Sheol and from the power of the godless: they will be raised up by God's power to share eternal joy with Christ Jesus. May God grant us this favor.

Beloved brothers and sisters, at any moment we expect the judges and executioners to come and inflict all kinds of suffering on us. We have resigned ourselves to it and expect nothing else.

May the Lord give us strength and faith to remain steadfast in His divine truth to the end, to witness to it and fight for it unto death. We hope to stimulate you and all brothers and sisters by our good example in serving God and following His Word. We wish to leave behind us, for the benefit of all men, a picture of uprightness and a good reputation for manliness. For this we fight and work very hard. May God in Heaven fulfill this longing and complete it in us through Christ.

The Lord is still adding daily to His holy Church those who are saved. The harvest is ripe and there is much work to do, but good laborers are very scarce. We need to call upon the Lord of the harvest, begging Him to send workers into His vineyard. Many of the people we were told about as seeking the truth do not amount to anything, and many we knew nothing about come forward and join us. One disciple awakens another; one discovers the other and leads him to God. There is so much of God's work for us to do, work with the brothers and sisters, with those seeking to find God, with children—work

Acts 2:47

Matt. 9:38 Luke 10:2

everywhere. We cannot do it all at once, and some things have to be left. But we will do as much as we can and will not spare ourselves. We are really needed everywhere at once; the urgency and greatness of the task weighs heavily upon us.

Brothers and sisters, I would have liked to write more, but I do not have time, and so I pass on to you now what I have hurriedly put on paper. So remember us faithfully before God every day.

As you know, Martin Nieder and Christel Bühler (Philler) fell away from God and His people and are excluded; they are now up here in Sterzing. They are godless, wicked men in alliance with the Devil. They have betrayed everything they know to the government at Innsbruck; they have told many terrible stories and lies and keep on doing it. They slander and blaspheme the truth of God. Of their sin quite a lot more could be said, but I will write more about that to the Servants. I will just say this: they plan to come to your area in a few days. They have no good intentions; they are only out to make trouble. Their designs are very evil. The enemies are partly responsible for this journey. So do not trust these men; they will come like thieves and murderers, sent out to rob, cheat, and kill. Beware!

Now I entrust you to God the Almighty, to His powerful protection, and to the Word of His grace. May He comfort and strengthen you, stand by you, and be with you always through our Jesus Christ both here and in Eternity.

The brothers and sisters here, the whole Church of God, greet all you beloved children of God a thousand times with the warm, brotherly love of their hearts, in the peace of the Lord and with the holy kiss of Jesus Christ. They long for you and wish they could see you face to face in the love of God. And I, Jakob, your Servant and apostle, your faithful brother and friend in the Lord (for I believe you love me), greet each one of you a thousand times. I write these words with my own hand in pure brotherly love and greet you with the true kiss of Jesus Christ. I embrace you with the arms of my heart. My thoughts are with you always. May God's peace and love and His Spirit be with you forever through Jesus Christ. Amen.

LETTER VII

Letter VII, carried to Moravia by brother Christel Schmidt in 1535, was written in response to letters and messages received in Tirol through brother Hänsel. At the serious risk of discovery, the believers held meetings over several days. The letters were read to all brothers and sisters present, and other matters were discussed. The Brotherhood celebrated the Lord's Supper while they were together; this seems to be the only mention of the Lord's Supper.

Hutter reports the capture of several believers (among them the daughter of a local judge) and the release of a sister who had been imprisoned for some time. Here too he comforts the suffering brothers and sisters in Moravia by calling to their minds many words from the Scriptures.

Beloved in Christ:

May God's grace and compassion, His eternal peace, blessing, and help, and the balm and consolation of the Holy Spirit from on High be with you brothers, and with all souls who suffer for their

faithfulness to Christ. May God comfort
and strengthen you from Heaven and
stand by you in your great need and distress. May He send heavenly wine for you
to drink, to strengthen you and give you
joy even in your troubles—that is the comfort of His Holy Spirit. May God be your
Captain, your Shield, your Stronghold
against all enemies! May He have mercy
on you and look upon you from Heaven
with compassionate eyes! In all His
dealings with you may He show His
omnipotence in signs and wonders, and
pour His mercy over you.

Ps.
18:2
Ps.
144:2

Matt.
24:22

O God of Heaven, shorten the days of
this great tribulation for the sake of Thy
chosen ones! Protect and strengthen Thy
holy people! Rescue them from the
enemies who set traps for their souls night
and day! God of Heaven, have pity on the
misery and pain of Thy suffering children!
Come, merciful Father, come soon, and
do not delay Thy help and compassion, for
the sake of Thy Son Jesus Christ and Thy
holy Name! Pity Thy people and have
them in Thy care.

We all need Thy divine counsel, the discernment and wisdom of Thy Holy Spirit, so we know what to do and what not to do and what will please Thee in Heaven. Give us understanding of how to live and act according to Thy will and pleasure, how to order and rule every part of our lives in fear of Thee and to Thy glory! Send Thy holy angels and guide us into all truth John 16:13 through the eternal light of Thy Holy Spirit. Lead us so that we bring Thee honor and glory and rich fruits in loyal service to Thee and Thy people. O God, come down and help Thy people. Keep us Ps. 144:5-7 safely in Thy care through Jesus Christ and His great mercy! Amen.

With all our heart we wish this for you who are chosen by the Lord, and we ask God for it every day and night. May God answer our prayer through His holy Name and through His Son Jesus Christ. Amen.

Dear brothers and sisters, we received your letter. God guided the brothers safely to us. We welcomed them joyfully and received all your messages eagerly and with great thankfulness in the fear of God—really in God's love. We read your letter aloud many times and listened to it carefully.

We never got tired of reading it. All the brothers and sisters here have heard it. We were eager to learn and to tell others about your faith and the great love you have for God and the brothers and about the persecution you are so patiently suffering. We have pondered all of this in our hearts, and it has brought us strength and comfort. We praise God now even more for you and for us. Glory be to Him Above, through Jesus Christ, for ever and ever. Amen.

Soon afterward came our dear brother Hänsel with another word from you. This letter I, Jakob, heard and read aloud to all God's children. We immediately called the whole Church together for a meeting that lasted two or three days. We proclaimed and spoke about the Word of God, and God protected and watched over us so that we could carry out His commands as we longed to do. We also held the Lord's Supper, celebrating it in power and truth. To God the Father be praise, honor, and everlasting thanks through Jesus Christ.

We want you to know all this, beloved brothers and sisters, so that your hearts may be comforted and cheered and you can glorify and praise God with us and gain confidence in the Lord in the midst of your distress. It was a wonderful gathering! God made it possible, though the danger was great. He is surely able to protect His own. Where He watches, His plan goes forward, and no one can prevent it. A house watched by Him is well protected. But we know that when God allows the enemies to have their way, when ^{Ps. 127:1} He himself does not watch and shelter, all our wisdom and caution is in vain.

Beloved children of the living God, our dear brothers and sisters, when we heard of your great suffering, pain, and poverty, a two-edged sword went right through our hearts. It was not our clothes that were rent but our very hearts that were torn open. We are grieved like unto death. We suffer with you and bear your anguish in our hearts. The news shocked us so greatly that we fell before God with bitter tears and poured out all our need to Him. We pray to Him unceasingly for you.

Dear ones, how I wish I could be with you in your wretchedness! But there is great need here too and very much to do for the Lord; there are many young branches of the Vine, scattered quite far apart, and many who are seeking the truth. We have more and more to do all the time. God in Heaven be praised for it all! Still, if only you had written or sent a message asking me to come, I do not think I would have let you down. I wish I could bear it all for you, even go into the grave for you for His Name's sake, if it were God's will. But with things as they are, I cannot do this responsibly in the fear of God and in the face of the need we have here. I am not even sure I would be able to help you, as matters now stand. However, if it were God's will and the will of all brothers and sisters, and if there were hope that I might be of help to you, I would gladly risk my life to come and save you.

Here we are in great distress too; persecution has begun, and there is a great outcry against us, although God has shown us a way out each day. At any moment we expect bailiffs and magistrates to discover us at several places. They have been threatening us, and they know quite well who the brothers and sisters are. God puts barriers in their way to keep them from coming, but humanly seen there is no time left—not a single day—judging by their threats.

The godless judge at Vintl, Peter Meier, has already imprisoned his own daughter, his son-in-law, and their maid—three of our dear ones. Like the cruel Leviathan, he opened wide his jaws and dragged them off to prison. The maid managed to get away from Schöneck Castle with her soul unsullied, true to God's will. She witnessed to the Lord faithfully and made no concessions. Though all three are young and have not yet received much teaching, they have been completely true, a delight to God and His people. We all can bear them witness. Also before their imprisonment they confessed the Lord faithfully in word and deed. Peter Meier's daughter said that with the Lord's help she would rather suffer death ten times over, if that were possible, than betray the truth. Still I cannot be absolutely certain that they will be steadfast to the end, nor can I call them blessed before they die; for only he who endures to the end will be saved. They are especially exposed to the Devil's temptation, since her husband is still held at Schöneck while she was taken to Greiffenburg in Carinthia, by her own brother, that villain Paul, whom the Devil has made her warden. So I am worried that she may stumble because of the great temptation she faces in her youthfulness and weakness. And yet I hope and trust that God the Almighty will not let them be lost forever but will graciously stretch out His hand and rescue them in His great compassion. Even so God helped the Apostle Peter and many believers. Scripture tells how God offered His merciful hand when they stumbled and fell through weakness or ignorance or because of much torture and temptation. We too have experienced this, when we were in great suffering.

Each of you must be on your guard and pay attention to what I write. Do not twist and misinterpret it, or you will be judged.

Matt.
10:22

Ps.
18:16,17
Ps.
138:7
Ps.
144:7

2 Pet.
3:16

You must not become lukewarm, relying on God's mercy and consoling yourselves with it. God might never again show you His mercy. Those who fear and serve God do not fall into this trap, but those who are irresponsible and godless provoke God in this way. The Scripture is like spears and nails to them; being blind they cannot understand it but only hurt themselves on it, wounding and defiling their own souls. They pervert and misinterpret Scripture, bringing their own condemnation; they remind us of what Job and the Apostles Paul and Peter say about the truth being falsified by the godless and the ignorant. With these words I warn each one, for such people will face a terrible judgment.

Job 13:3-5
Gal. 1:7
2 Thess. 2:11,12
2 Tim. 2:18

I want you to know, beloved in the Lord, that God heard our prayer. He freed our dear sister Nändl, who had been in prison a long time for His sake, and through brother Walser He led her to us. She remained faithful to the Lord, confessed loyally to Him at all times and witnessed to the divine truth in her words and way of living. Her soul is unstained, and in this purity she came to us.

Now you know everything about our present situation.

We would gladly have sent brother Hänsel back to you right away as you asked; we too thought it was necessary. But we did not send him because, as I already wrote, we called a meeting of the Church that lasted several days because we had many things to deal with, matters concerning God's work. Brother Hänsel was at some of these meetings, but not all the brothers were there; some were out visiting other brothers and sisters. I was simply not able to write because there was so much that needed to be done. Besides, Hänsel was quite exhausted from his traveling; he was here only a day when he fell ill with fever. So we did not dare send him this time for fear he would collapse on the way. But we hope he will soon be well again. Apart from that, God brought him safely to us, and he found us right away.

For these reasons, beloved brothers and sisters, I am now sending you as quickly as possible another brother, brother Christel. And if God our Father wills it, I plan to send Hänsel or another brother after him to bring you further news, whatever God gives me to write.

Therefore, most dearly beloved brothers and sisters, I ask you not to worry but to put your trust completely in God the Almighty. I know He will not forsake you or any who fear Him. He will show you His mercy and power and will help you in this need. Lift up your heads to God, you believers, for your redemption is drawing near with great power. The destruction and undoing of all the godless is also approaching. So turn completely from the world; beware of its evil words and works. Do not long for its life and pleasures or the Lord will condemn and destroy you along with it. He will reject you here, and in Eternity you will be cast into the abyss. The wickedness and arrogance of the godless is heaped as high as Heaven, before God's very countenance, as the Apostle John says, so that God can no longer endure the sight of it.

Therefore the Holy Spirit says, "Flee away, come out of her, my people, lest you share in her plagues." Oh, do not allow

Luke 21:28

Rev. 18:5

Rev. 18:4

yourselves to be misled or frightened away from God's truth! Whoever remains constant in it to the end shall be saved. Whoever fights manfully, patiently bearing all pain and temptation; whoever stands up for the Lord and praises Him before all men; whoever serves God and His people obediently till death, overcoming his own flesh, the Devil, and the whole world—God will crown with a fair garland that never withers. He will raise him from the dead and give him an immortal body like the glorified body of our Lord Jesus Christ. God will clothe him with a white robe.

Then the elect will shine like the sun in their Father's Kingdom, in the eternal Jerusalem, in the throne of glory. And God will wipe all tears from their faces and will take away all their pain. He will give them unspeakable joy, and it shall never be taken away from them, as the Scriptures say in many places. After their great suffering God will give them a thousand times greater comfort. All who have suffered grief and pain with Jerusalem (that is, with God's children) will be given eter-

1 Cor.
9:25
1 Pet.
5:4

Phil.
3:21
1 John
3:2

Rev.
6:11;
7:9

2 Esd.
7:97
Matt.
13:43

Isa.
25:8
Rev.
7:17
Rev.
21:4
2 Esd.
7:90,
91,98

Rom.
8:18

Isa.
66:10
Rom.
8:17

nal peace, joy, and inexpressible glory.
The chosen ones will eat and drink and
rejoice with all their hearts. They will lack
nothing. They will completely forget their
suffering, so great will be their jubilation!

The ungodly, however, will weep and
howl with great fear in their hearts; they
will lament in great torment; they will suffer from hunger and thirst and all kinds of
privation; they will be trampled upon like
dirt; they will be banished from the land of
the living, even from God the Lord
himself, and will be swept into Hell for
ever and ever. The prophets and all of
Scripture tell us this.

Isa.
13:6-13
Matt.
13:41,42
Rev.
21:8

But you may rejoice, brothers, and be
comforted, for your King and Savior,
Jesus Christ the Son of God, is coming.
He will soon appear on the clouds of
Heaven with hosts of angels, in great
power and glory. He will take vengeance
on all His foes and will redeem His chosen,
saving them from their enemies and from
every calamity. Those who have been
persecuted for His sake and have suffered
much, who have served Him and
acknowledged Him in the face of this evil

Matt.
24:30

generation, who have been obedient and
faithful to Him and to His people till
death—all these God the Lord will raise
up from the earth where they sleep, those
who have been murdered or have passed
away since the world's beginning. He will
take them into Heaven with Him and the

1 Thess.
4:17

heavenly hosts. They will all be caught up
into the clouds to meet the Lord, to be
with Him in all Eternity. God will give
them an everlasting Kingdom where

Dan.
2:44
Luke
1:32,33

Christ will sit upon the throne of David,
and of that Kingdom there will be no end.
They will have peace and joy; they will

Rev.
21:2
2 Tim.
2:12
Rev.
22:5

praise and glorify God in the new
Jerusalem and will live and reign with God
and Christ Jesus and all the heavenly hosts
for ever and ever.

May God the Father help us all to reach
this goal, through Jesus Christ; may He
guide us to that day through His holy
Name and great mercy! Console each
other with these words and be courageous,
you faithful ones, for God will give you
everlasting comfort.

In closing my letter I entrust you to our
merciful God and Father and to His Word

of grace. May He be with you and give you strength, love, and faith to bear all your need with patience. May He comfort you with the Holy Spirit and fill your hearts with His heavenly treasure. May God himself be your Captain, Shield, and For- ^{Ps.} tress. May He provide for you in body and soul out of His riches, with heavenly gifts as well as earthly ones, giving you what is good and necessary. This is the longing of our hearts for you. May this be the Father's will in His great mercy through Jesus Christ. Amen.

I also ask all you beloved ones to pray to the Lord God for us night and day, and we will do the same for you. We know that you are doing this, for we can feel it in many ways. Still we want to encourage you not to weaken, but instead to grow more and more persistent and faithful in your prayers.

You faithful Servants of the holy Church of God, Shepherds and Overseers, and every one of God's children in Moravia (wherever you may be in your misery, poverty, and fear), all the brothers and sisters of the Church here greet you with hearts full of burning, brotherly love and with the holy kiss of our Jesus Christ. The brothers Casper, Kränzler, Walser, Stoffel, and Hänsel (and also I, your brother Jeronimus) greet each one of you, and so do the sisters Nändl, Klärle, and my wife Traindel.[1] Greetings are also sent by the faithful members of this household where we have stayed the longest, whose names we will not write down for obvious reasons.

And I, Jakob, your apostle and Servant, your faithful brother and friend through God's grace, greet you, all you dear Servants of the Lord and all brothers and sisters, wherever you may be. I greet every single one of you a thousand times in brotherly love from my whole heart; I embrace you with the arms of my heart and kiss you with the holy kiss and in the peace of our Jesus Christ. May my heart, soul, and spirit be with you always. May you be with me, we with God, and God with us all forever, through the great mercy of Jesus Christ.

[1] This shows clearly that Jakob Hutter dictated these letters, in this case to Jeronimus Käls.

Beloved brothers and sisters, members of the Body of Jesus Christ, how we long to be able to help you in your distress, to show you love and honor, to give you shelter, food, and drink, to comfort and strengthen you! Oh, may God grant us this privilege! What rejoicing there would be in our hearts! How eagerly we would do this in love, putting at your service our bodies, lives, and goods, all the heavenly and earthly gifts we have received from God. We would be willing to endure much suffering to make this possible. No amount of pain and torment could stop us. May everything happen according to God's will and for His eternal praise and glory! May you be in His care through Jesus Christ. Amen.

From me, Jakob, a servant of the Lord and His holy Church, and from all the children of God scattered in the Puster and Adige valleys, who are your brothers and companions in the Lord. We share ^{Rev. 1:9} patiently with you in tribulation and in Christ's Kingdom. Amen. Amen in Eternity.

LETTER VIII

Carried from Tirol to Moravia in 1535 by Jeronimus Käls, Letter VIII begins with Jakob Hutter's clear witness to his calling from God. He exhorts the brothers and sisters to remain true under persecution and comforts them with God's promises of the glory to come.

Reported in this letter is the imposition of even stricter measures against the Anabaptists in Tirol, intended to stamp them out altogether. Many were imprisoned and all in great danger and distress. Jakob Hutter himself was captured soon afterward (the official record in Brixen is dated December 1, 1535), and the unusual longing and warmth to be felt in this letter indicate his awareness of extreme danger.

This letter is sent to God's chosen children, guests and pilgrims on this earth for the sake of the Lord, to you our beloved brothers and sisters who are suffering greatly and are scattered all over Moravia.

God in His unspeakable mercy has chosen me, Jakob, to be His helper, an apostle of Jesus Christ, and a servant of all His children, those here in the mountains of Tirol and those in Moravia. He has chosen and fitted me for this task though I in no way deserve it, only because of His overflowing goodness. He has made me worthy to serve Him in the everlasting Covenant He established with Abraham and his seed. He has placed His Word in my heart and mouth. He entrusted to me the riches of His Holy Spirit, which lie hidden in the dwelling place of God, the King over all kings. He has given me His blessing. He has made His Word alive in me and in many to whom I proclaimed His will, sealing it through the working of His Holy Spirit with mighty miracles and signs. He has made me a watchman and shepherd of His people, His holy Church. She is the Bride of our beloved Jesus Christ, bought and purified with His precious blood. He has given me many faithful Christian souls and is still doing so.

Ezek.
3:17

For all these things may God the heavenly Father, the King and Creator of all, be praised, blessed, and honored. I praise and thank Him in His eternal majesty from the bottom of my heart. May all the believers and heavenly hosts exalt Him forevermore, through Jesus Christ. Amen.

You are called to be fighters and witnesses of God and of our Lord Jesus Christ. You are my beloved brothers and sisters. You are my longed-for children, whom I bore and planted with much labor through God's Word and heavenly grace. In your distress, fear, and need, in the persecution you suffer for the Lord's sake, I wish all of you from the depth of my heart God's grace and peace and His eternal life. I wish you much love and faith and strength to overcome the world. May God comfort you and give you your daily bread, caring for you in body and soul with heavenly and temporal gifts. May He help and support you through His presence, and protect you in all Eternity.

You children of God, although we know a good deal about your difficult situation

1 Cor. 4:15
1 Cor. 3:6

and are keenly aware of the tribulation and persecution you suffer for the Lord's sake, we have not heard from you what has happened recently. We think of you constantly. Your distress strikes our hearts, and we bear your suffering with you, as well as what we have to bear here in Tirol for the Lord's sake. We continually pray to God for you who have been implanted in our hearts. You are a living letter written by God's love and Spirit, a letter we read over and over.

2 Cor.
3:2,3

You beloved ones, some time ago I sent our brother Christel to you. I wrote to tell you how things are with us here and to comfort you in the way God showed me.[1] I hope you received that message. I would send our brother Hänsel right away, as you asked, and he would gladly come to you, urged by the love we all feel toward you. But this is not possible now because he is ill. I cannot even use him here at the moment, though he and more brothers are badly needed, since we are in great distress too, as you will hear. Still, because of my

---

[1]This refers to Letter VII, delivered by Christel Schmidt.

great love for you, I will send our dear
brother Jeronimus to you in your need. I
would rather suffer even greater want
myself to be able to lessen yours.

If only we could help you in your need
in the way we long to, if only we could do
enough for you to satisfy our hearts! O
that our heavenly Father might grant our
hearts' desire, because of the joy we have
in you, to take you in and help you in your
distress, to shelter you and give you food
and drink, and to show you our love and
faithfulness—to honor you with both
spiritual and temporal nourishment. How
we would rejoice in the Holy Spirit! We
could wish for no greater privilege. It is
our greatest sorrow not to be able to see
you and do all this for you. We would so
gladly endure poverty and suffering, pain
and torture and even death, for the sake of
being united with you at this time and
serving in all ways. Our hearts lie open
before you.

O children of God, your misery pains
me deeply! My heart is full of compassion
for you in the trials you suffer for His
sake. But be comforted, you faithful ones,

and remember that this happened to all the prophets, to Christ the Lord himself, and to all His apostles, to all who were chosen and loved by God the Lord since the beginning of the world.

You have heard this often and it is pointed out again and again in the Scriptures. God the Lord has clearly shown that until the Day of Judgment suffering will always come upon those who love His truth. And think of how often and how seriously I spoke to you about this while I was still with you, even before it happened. Some did not recognize God's goodness and compassion, so He had to make them recognize it through suffering. Some were not thankful to the Lord, and many of these have already been revealed and separated from us. But let all who love and fear God recognize His fatherly will and the riches of His mercy even in these trials. Let them be a reminder to us never to forget Him or become ungrateful to Him, never to grow sleepy or negligent in serving Him. Let us never allow our flesh to gain the upper hand and rule us; let us never fall prey to sin, indulge in worldly pleasures, or let earthly lusts defile us.

Our suffering should help us to crucify our flesh with its passions and desires. Then our inner man will be strengthened by the Holy Spirit, who will guide us into all truth, and we will come to know God the Lord and His mercy more fully. Let us praise and glorify Him and serve Him from our hearts with fear and trembling. Suffering should make us grow in love and faith, in righteousness and truth, and help us to reach the perfection God promises and gives to His own. Let us not become like a dry, unfruitful tree that will be burned on the unquenchable fire, but like a lovely, green olive tree, yielding the Lord good fruits. Let us not waste the time we still have on earth, doing only what our flesh desires, but let us serve and obey God and His children as long as we live.

The Lord disciplines us because we are His children. In the Apostle Peter's words: Whoever suffers in the flesh has ceased to sin. For the rest of his life he no longer serves the world and his own flesh, no longer lives for sin or by his own will. While his pilgrimage lasts, he lives for God

Margin references: Gal. 5:24 · Eph. 3:16 · John 16:13 · Matt. 3:10 · Matt. 7:19 · Ecclus. 50:10 · 1 Pet. 4:1,2 · Rom. 6:6-13

and devotes his life to the praise of God in obedience to the brothers. Through suffering God cleanses us of the world and of all created things, so that in our hearts we break with it all and turn with our whole will to Him alone. That means putting our entire confidence in Him, knowing that He is our comfort. We will follow His eternal Word and keep His Law night and day and will find our joy and delight in the Lord. We will love God, the Lord in Heaven, and His children with all our heart and all our soul and all our strength. Our treasure will be in Heaven alone.

Deut.
6:5
Matt.
22:37
Luke
10:27

Everything that is happening now comes to us from God the Almighty, from His great love and compassion, so that we may not be condemned with the world but live with Him and gain peace, joy, and eternal life in His Kingdom. Otherwise our flesh would rule us and lead us into sin, and the wages of sin is eternal death. Those who are carnal cannot please God. As Scripture says, fleshly and sinful people will not inherit the Kingdom of God. In the Book of Proverbs is written, "Wounds

I Cor.
11:32

Rom.
6:23

Gal.
5:21

Prov.
20:30

and blows drive evil from the body," meaning that sin is driven out by the Cross of Jesus Christ, which is the Lord's rod. Job 9:34

So take comfort, you beloved chosen ones, for all this is a sure sign that you are dear to God and that He will give you eternal life. Eternal life means peace, joy, and glory with all who have gone before and with the whole heavenly host. May God the Father help us all to win the prize Phil. 3:14 through His Son Jesus Christ, to whom be praise and honor forever. Amen.

Dear children of the living God, through the Spirit, I have long had in my heart a foreboding of this distress and terror. I warned you day and night of its coming, teaching you to prepare your hearts to accept suffering. I taught you to cling to God alone and not let fear drive you away from His truth and His Church. Remain true until the end, through all affliction. For whoever endures to the end Matt. 24:13 will be saved. Fight to the death for the Ecclus. 4:28 truth, and the Lord God will fight for you. Be steadfast and patient in your service to Him and to the brothers.

I have pleaded with you to listen to God's Word with earnest attention and to let it be imprinted in your hearts. We will not always be with you and able to speak to you; God may take us from you through imprisonment, persecution, or death, in whatever way He may ordain. Then in times of trouble you will have something to sustain you. You must

Prov.
6:8
Prov.
10:5

gather in while it is summer, so that in the cold and dangerous winter time you are clothed and provided for and can draw from your hearts' store the treasures you have received from God. How many times in the past I explained this to you! I wish you had understood it deeply. The Word of truth has been proclaimed to you quite clearly and shown to you by the many powerful examples of what God has done with His children. Happy are those who heard it all and took it into their hearts!

Exod.
13:21,22
Num.
14:14
Neh.
9:12,19

You also know that for a long time the Lord went before you in a pillar of cloud by day, that is, through His Servants. But night will come and you will no longer be able to see the cloud; then the Lord will go before His own in a pillar of fire. This pillar of fire is the Word that lives in all true Christian hearts, working in them and guiding them to the truth and to a firm faith. God will lead them with the radiance of His Holy Spirit and through His Word. Happy is the man who has this radiant, shining light to guide him; he will not come to grief at night. Scripture says, "The just shall live by faith, and shall never be put to shame." _{Hab. 2:4}

Take care then, brothers and sisters, and consider it seriously in your hearts, for the hour is here, and all you were told in the Lord's Name is happening. Happy the man who has heard and received God's Word, who has love and faith, patience, righteousness, and truth in his heart, who fears God, and who lives by the Holy Spirit. He will remain faithful in this misery.

Beloved brothers and sisters, it may be that I or other Servants of God will not be able to speak to you again in this world, never again set eyes on you in this life, or be able to comfort and strengthen you with words of truth. So see to it that you do not waver, but with all your hearts firmly trust in God the Lord. Always be ready to do His will and keep His commandments; witness to God in your words and deeds, in your whole way of life. Let your light shine before men, so that your good works can be seen and God the Father is glorified through you. Then Christ will acknowledge you in the presence of His Father and before the angels in Heaven. He will call you His sons and daughters, His brothers and sisters, fellow heirs of His glory, and children of the living God.

If you love God and His people, then you will be loved by Him, by His Son, and by all believers. If you serve God the Lord and His children with your whole heart, then the angels in Heaven will serve you. If you do not forget the Lord's Word, then God the Lord will never forget you. And if you abide in God and His truth and in community with all the chosen, then God the Lord will abide in you forever and will never forsake you.

Keep in mind that what we taught you came from God's grace as a gift, from

Matt. 5:16

Matt. 10:32
Luke 12:8

Rom. 8:17

God's Word and the Holy Spirit; everyone should be eager to obey it. We did not tell you fables or fairy tales; what we preached was not based on human ideas but on God's truth, which will never pass away. It is the Word of divine justice, pure and clearly established before God and all the chosen. We are sure of this, for we received it from God himself. This Word is testified to in the Holy Scriptures and sealed by the blood of many believers, and with God's help we too hope to bear witness to the truth with our blood. *2 Pet. 1:16*

This is the right door to the sheepfold; it is the true faith, the foundation that all the prophets and apostles built on. This is what we taught you. Let no one tell you otherwise. Anyone who teaches you anything else is cursed, as Paul the Apostle writes. Before God these men are all thieves and murderers. And a thief comes only to steal and to kill. *John 10:7* *Gal. 1:8,9* *John 10:8* *John 10:10*

We do not live in error or teach falsehoods, nor do we sway back and forth like a reed in the wind. With God's help, no amount of suffering or temptation will shake us. No torture or pain, hunger or *Matt. 11:7* *Luke 7:24* *Rom. 8:35-39* thirst, trouble or persecution, no man or any other creature or thing that can be named shall lead us astray or separate us from God and His divine truth. For the word we preach and live by is established and sealed by God through His chosen with powerful signs, as I said before. And we are not bringing anything new to your ears; we are not fickle, saying one thing today and another tomorrow, like those who are irresponsible and false. We will remain firm and immovable in the divine truth forever, cost what it may. What we preached from the beginning we still preach and are not weary or ashamed. This should encourage you to be bold and manly and brave for the Lord.

How I wish, you faithful ones, that I could be with you for just one day or a single hour and let my voice be heard among you. How my soul would be refreshed and my heart find joy in the Lord! But that does not seem to be God's plan, and we accept His will patiently, though with great sorrow.

Be comforted, you elect of the Lord, for

Acts
14:3

Phil.
4:4

the time of our deliverance is close. Lift up _{Luke} _{21:28}
your heads and wait patiently, firm in love
and faith and righteousness and truth, for
your Shepherd and King is near. He that is
coming will come soon. He will come on _{Matt.} _{24:30}
the clouds of Heaven with great power and
glory, the King and Comforter of Israel.
He will redeem His own, and on their _{2 Esd.} _{2:43,46}
heads He will set a glorious and unfading _{1 Pet.} _{5:4}
crown. But before this there will be _{Rev.} _{2:10}
struggle and strife. Whoever is victorious
in this fight through God's Spirit will be _{1 Cor.} _{9:24,25}
crowned; he will win the prize and be given _{2 Esd.} _{7:91-98}
peace and joy and everlasting glory with
the faithful and all the heavenly host. He
will be with God the Father and His dear
Son and will abide with them forever
according to the covenant of eternal life.
May God help us all reach this through
Jesus Christ. To Him be praise and honor
from everlasting to everlasting.

I am comforted by God's promise to us
that we shall behold Him in His holy _{Rev.} _{22:4}
Temple, that our distress shall come to an _{Rev.} _{7:15-17}
end one day and our weeping cease, and _{Rev.} _{21:4}
that we shall see each other again with
great joy. And no one will hurt or abuse us

anymore, for all suffering will pass away. In power, the Lord will tear off the veils that represent earthly power and might. Then the faithful shall reign, and their mouths shall be full of laughter. They will rejoice in the Lord and together sing praises to Him eternally.

May God help us to wait expectantly for His grace and His perfect compassion; then we will receive joy a thousand times greater than all our sorrow and misery. In this world we have no rest or permanent home, only sorrow, fear, and pain. But be comforted, for Christ has overcome the world, and He will give us grace and strength so that we too may overcome it. He conquered for our sake, so that the same victory may be given to us and to all who truly fear and love God, who keep His commandments and believe in Him with their whole hearts. For the true and living Christian faith is the victory that overcomes the world. May God our heavenly Father give you His comfort in all your tribulation. How I wish it were God's will for me to be with you and you with me! I would a thousand times rather

Ezek.
13:21

2 Tim.
2:12
Rev.
22:5
Ps.
126:2

Heb.
13:14

John
16:33

1 John
5:4

suffer with you in deepest distress, even in great torture and pain, than share the pleasure and luxury of the ungodly. But I am comforted by the Lord that even if this cannot happen now, still we shall be united in Eternity.

Beloved ones, my heart, soul, and spirit will be with you at all times, and I know you are with me. May God be with all of us, and we with God forevermore! With this I entrust you to the powerful protection of the Lord God in Heaven and of Jesus Christ the Great Shepherd. May He strengthen you and supply your every need Phil. 4:19 with His heavenly and temporal gifts, according to His will and according to the riches of His great mercy. May He protect you for ever and ever. Amen.

Beloved brothers and sisters, about ourselves I can say that we are living in love and faith and in the peace and unity of the Holy Spirit. In our hearts is great pain and sorrow for your sake, and outwardly we are suffering severe persecution. The horrible, raging dragon has opened its Rev. 12:1,3,4 jaws wide to devour the woman robed with the sun. She is the Church and the Bride of Jesus Christ.

After our meeting on Sunday, a brother from Tauffers was captured on his way home. Soon afterward, the judge of Brixen rode into the village of Lüsen, summoned all the men, women, and children able to walk, and read out to them a cruel mandate that forbade them to house or shelter any of us. If anyone did, he would be punished more severely than ever, and his house would be burned to the ground. The judge said that this thing was spreading and getting out of hand and that the Prince-Bishop of Brixen would not tolerate it but would root it right out. He has just returned home and now threatens the people with big words, forbidding what is good and right and commanding what is evil. However, the believers are still courageous and pay no attention to his threats, but serve God eagerly and do His will.

The judge would have held off for a while to see whether we would let ourselves be intimidated and take part in their blasphemous idol-worship, and he would willingly have closed one eye for a while. But our betrayers would not leave him in peace. Our brothers and sisters are already known to everybody in the valley and round about.

When the judge saw that his orders had no effect on us, he set out and captured five or six brothers and sisters, and took them to Brixen. God protected the others that time; but we have just now been informed by an unbeliever that five more have been taken from Lüsen to Brixen. We have not heard any more, but there is good reason to worry about what is happening to them and how they are faring. At this point we do not know where they are imprisoned, but God in Heaven knows. I immediately sent brothers to Lüsen and all around to visit the brothers and sisters and find out how they are. They have not returned yet, so I really do not know how matters stand. But it is very likely that all have been chased out and scattered and that they are in great danger wherever they are.

So far, everything we have heard about the prisoners and all the others points to their steadfastness and faithfulness.[1] May God comfort them with the Holy Spirit and strengthen them with His Word. May He keep them in His Name to the end. May He stand by their side through Jesus Christ to help and support them in His great mercy. Amen.

Our brother Jeronimus will surely tell you what our situation is and whatever else there is to report. He is as well informed about everything as I am at the moment and knows what you need to be told. He is our living letter to you and will answer all your questions. For the rest, let us all wait patiently for the Lord.

2 Cor. 3:2,3

In closing, we ask you for the sake of God's mercy to pray for us persistently, as we do for you. We know that you are doing this, only do not slacken; rather increase your efforts, for we urgently need your prayers. I know that God will provide a way out for His own, as He has promised in His great compassion. May God be with us and with you, may He

1 Cor. 10:13

2 Cor. 1:4

[1]According to court records the judge took ten captives from Lüsen (Southern Tirol) to Brixen. (M.E. III, p. 415)

comfort all grieving souls with the comfort of His Holy Spirit.

All of God's children here, the whole Church, greet you very faithfully from their hearts and with the kiss of our Lord Jesus Christ; they greet each one of you a thousand times in the love and peace of God. And I, Jakob, your Servant, your brother and companion in the suffering of Jesus Christ—I too greet you all together and each one personally, every Servant and brother and sister, in warm brotherly love from a peaceful heart and with the holy kiss of our Jesus. May God the Father in Heaven, who is all grace and mercy, comfort and bless you with His Holy Spirit, through Jesus Christ in all Eternity. Amen.

Rev. 1:9

You beloved and chosen ones, we give our body, soul, and spirit to the Lord and to you. Be assured of our love, and take courage in the Lord! May God keep us in His love and in the covenant of His peace forever. Amen.

LETTER IX

Although the authorship of this valuable testimony, the second letter to the government of Moravia, is uncertain (see Appendix C), we include it in this collection because it is a clear and convincing statement of the position of the Church that bore Jakob Hutter's name, particularly on the questions of government authority, taxes, military service, and the right of assembly.

After the community was driven away from Auspitz in 1535, the brothers and sisters lived in small scattered groups, hiding in the fields and forests or secretly employed by lesser nobles. By 1537 persecution lessened and Bruderhofs could be established again on various estates.

This letter was sent in 1545 to correct the false accusations that had reached the ears of the authorities (largely through unfaithful Brotherhood members) and to give a true picture of the life and beliefs of the Brotherhood.

We are brothers and true followers of our Lord and Master Jesus Christ. In His great mercy and compassion, the Almighty gathered us from many different countries, especially from the German-speaking countries.

We are called to the light of divine truth, which has been shed upon all men in our time. So having turned away from our sinful way of life, we wish from now on to serve in steadfast and genuine righteousness before God, who has led us here and gathered us together.

Luke
1:74,75

We wish you the same experience that God has given us, the knowledge of God and His everlasting truth, through Jesus Christ.

You, the Lords of Moravia, should know that we came from many districts and princedoms to this country only because we recognized the truth and wish to serve God faithfully. Many other countries prevented us from doing this by the cruel tyranny of their governments. They took by force what was ours and drove us from our houses. They imprisoned many of our members for long periods, and even worse, put many of them to death.

1 Cor.
4:11-13

But because God the Lord in His mercy long ago chose a place for us to gather, in order to serve Him and grow in faith, we have accepted this from Him with great thankfulness. All of us whose hearts are moved by God and His Word have gathered and are determined to serve God, with His help. We want to walk blamelessly before God with a good conscience and glorify Him through our faithfulness; this has always been our aim.

1 Tim. 1:5

There is, however, an angry outcry against us from irresponsible people, especially from those who have left us, forsaking the truth and making friends with the world again. They spread evil reports about us, which must have reached your ears. But we know we are quite innocent of their accusations.

2 Tim. 4:3,4
Rom. 1:24-32

Most of you may not know much about our way of life, though some do know the truth about us very well. The whole country is full of complaints that have been made against us and malicious talk spread by those who turned against the truth in their evil rebellion. They have become our wholehearted enemies. These slanders have confused you, causing you to doubt us and to think there must be something to it even if it is not the whole story.

So we want to give you an account of our teaching and way of life. We feel accountable to you and to all men, especially with regard to certain questions: the right of assembly, government authority, and taxes. We heard that you are especially interested in these points.

First, the foundation of our faith is this: we believe in one, eternal, life-giving God, who made Heaven and earth and sea, and everything living in them. He maintains life in all He has created on the earth. He rules over the hearts of men and establishes His righteousness in them. In Him we believe.

By the Word of His truth He has given us rebirth as children of God, through Jesus Christ. We believe that Jesus Christ is one with God the Father, from whom He came forth in power; He became man through the virgin Mary, truly was born as a man on this earth: He was sent to save all sinners who repent and turn to God so that they may be reconciled with the Father.

We believe that Jesus Christ, by suffering death Himself, robbed Death of his power. He ascended into Heaven and sits at the right hand of the Father to intercede for us.

We believe that Jesus Christ has fulfilled the promise of the Father in pouring out His Spirit upon us, His believers. This Spirit proceeds from the Father and the Son, and we believe that He is one essence and power with them. Still today the Spirit gathers people into His Church, the Church of Christ. He leads them to serve God with one mind and one heart and makes the Word of truth live in them. Those who live faithfully in God's sight to the end will inherit eternal life and rejoice in His peace.

Next we want to explain our attitude to the government of this country, how far we should obey it and how far we recognize it as being given by God.

To this point we say that there must be government authority in the world, and

I Pet.
2:13-17

that it has been ordained by God for the punishment of evildoers and for the reward of those who do good. So anyone who refuses to obey the government in reasonable matters, or maintains that it has no right to exist, is opposing God's order. Therefore we will readily obey it in all we recognize to be just in the eyes of God, for instance paying taxes and other dues. But God has not given the government power to demand obedience of us in matters that conflict with our conscience. Then we say with the Apostle Peter that

Acts
5:29

we must obey God rather than man. Many of you knew this when we first came to settle in this country, and you proved your fear of God by not expecting us to do anything against our conscience.

But recently some unfaithful brothers, who want a life of ease and favor with men rather than with God and have forsaken God in their hearts, have ingratiated themselves with the authorities and told them just what they wanted to hear, for instance, that we should be paying war taxes or other ungodly things. They had no right from God to slander the brothers, putting heavily on the believers' shoulders the burden of the cross they themselves had cast off. And they did this knowing that once the brothers are scattered, their own wickedness need not be brought to light and would go unpunished.

It was the same in earlier times, when those Israelites who rebelled were Israel's worst enemies. They caused the greatest affliction by stirring up the authorities against their own people, so that the Israelites could not find shelter in the land.

I Kings 12:19
2 Chron. 10:19

The same story is told in the Books of the Maccabees. The godless Jason and other wicked men aroused the pagan authorities (who had never been favorably inclined toward the faithful) and misled the Lord's people. All who followed their lead, seducing the faithful, sinned heavily and brought judgment upon their own heads.

2 Macc. 4:7-10

Another dreadful example is Antiochus "the noble." But Antiochus is not the only example; there were many others, kings and generals. One of these was Sennacherib, who according to God's plan was murdered by his sons in the temple of

I Macc. 1:20-24

2 Kings 19:37

his god Nisroch; similarly, Haman was hanged on the gallows he had prepared for Mordecai; and Sisera, Nicanor, and many more lost their lives in the villainous traps they had set for others.

In this way God proves that He is the Protector of His people and that anyone who persecutes God's people will be punished. He warns all men by His Spirit not to lay hands upon His anointed or maltreat His servants and prophets; for, says the Lord, "Whoever harms you lays violent hands upon the apple of my eye."

With regard to the taxes that you are given the right to demand, we say the following: We owe you obedience in this matter. In the world, just as among the believers, all authority comes from God, who is the Overseer of all men. He ordered that the inhabitants of any country (all who make use of the services of the State) should pay taxes. Taxes help to maintain these services and support the authorities, so that the government is able to carry out its appointed tasks, and anyone who refuses is resisting God.

Marginal references:
Esther 7:10
Judg. 4:12-22
1 Macc. 7:47
Deut. 30:7
Zech. 2:8,9
Matt. 22:17-21
Mark 12:14-17

The authorities of any place we have lived in know perfectly well and can report that we have never refused to pay any of the yearly contributions demanded of us. For the sake of the Lord God we have been obedient subjects of the human order He established.

But if anything is demanded of us that goes beyond God's command or is opposed to Him or not ordained by Him, we must refuse; that is the case with war taxes or executioners' taxes or other things a Christian may not take part in. These things have no foundation in the Scriptures; they are repugnant to God and to the nature of His Son, who came not to destroy the souls of men but to save them. He taught us not to return blow for blow, *Matt.* not to take revenge for evil suffered on our *5: 38-40,* own persons, but rather to return good for *44,48* evil and to do good to our enemies and in this way show forth the nature of our Father in Heaven. Therefore it is impossible for us to do any of these things. The liar will be punished as well as the thief; it is as clear as day that whoever contributes money to pay the soldiers is as guilty as the soldier who kills others.

For this reason we do not take vengeance or seek human protection, but for all things we turn to God. In accordance with His Word we leave vengeance to Him, who at His own time will save us from all our enemies. But we praise and thank God that it never entered our heads to act like the Münsterites, although we are constantly accused of being like them.[1] Instead we give thanks to the Son, who said, "Blessed are you when men revile you and persecute you and say all manner of evil against you, if they are lying. Rejoice and be glad, for great is your reward in heaven." Anyone who knows us can see that nobody is less like the Münsterites than we are, since there is nothing we hate more than bloodshed. We declare publicly that violence is the work of the Devil and not of God. The Devil has always been the prince of war and bloodshed.

Heb.
10:30

Matt.
5:11,12

---

[1]The Münsterites were Anabaptists who took up arms under John of Leyden to establish a "New Jerusalem" in the city of Münster. They ruled it from 1533 to 1535 with violence and licentiousness, and the tragedy that ensued did great harm to the Anabaptist cause throughout history.

The Bible is often quoted to excuse warfare. People say that David and many others waged war. We answer that in Old Testament times the new Kingdom of Christ had not yet been revealed. In this Kingdom the scepter of power and the weapons of war are spiritual, not made of iron. And God commands us now to beat our swords into plowshares and sickles. Wars must cease throughout the world wherever believers are.

Eph. 6:13-17

Isa. 2:4

War was not wrong for David and other devout men who lived before the time when grace was fully poured out by God. But to all those who have been chosen by God, war is now forbidden. Christ said, "You have heard that it was said of old, 'An eye for an eye, a head for a head, a hand for a hand,' but that is not what I say." Also, "Of old it was said, 'Thou shalt love thy neighbor and hate thine enemy,' but I say to you, 'Love your enemies, do good to them that injure you, and pray for your persecutors.'" Christ did not say, "Go to war against them with the sword." Therefore we would not even think of

Matt. 5:38,39

Matt. 5:43,44

doing so, for we want to be children of our Father in Heaven. And just as we are forbidden to return evil for evil or to fight against our enemies, we are forbidden to pay war taxes. In God's eyes the one is just as wrong as the other.

We do not oppose these things out of wickedness or self-will, but only because we fear God and do not want our hearts to be burdened with any wrong. We would rather die than injure even our worst enemies. That is why we will not pay war taxes or destroy human life.

Regarding our community, our gathering of people, we heard that we will not be tolerated any longer, that we are an affront to the King and his princes. This might be partly because there are so many of us. It might also be because we are suspected of being like the Münsterites, but as we already said, that has never entered our minds, and we hope it never will. But the main reason we are misunderstood is made clear to us by the words of Jesus. It is because we walk in the truth. The world does not accept the truth

but has always loved darkness more than John 3:19
light. So it does not surprise us that we are
hated for our witness to love, truth, and
unity. For Christ says, "If you were of the John 15:19
world, the world would love you. Because
you are not of the world, but I chose you
out of the world, the world hates you." We
know that the way we are called to, this
way of gathering and living together, is
from God. We did not invent it. He
Himself established it through the Holy
Spirit to make Himself known to the Col. 1:27
world, to reveal to men the working of His
merciful will.

Since God commanded this through His
Spirit working within us, we could not
take His bidding lightly and ask first
whether it was right. We surrendered
ourselves completely to His will in order to
make room for His truth in us. Just as in
the early Church, He made us of one heart Acts 4:32
and one soul in the name of Jesus Christ.
He led us together to serve Him in unity
and to show that God himself is one and Mark 12:29 Gal. 3:20
undivided.

The world with its darkened conscience
cannot recognize God or His nature. But

contrary to all worldly cleverness and human reasoning, God has led His people and given them new hearts so that no one any longer seeks his own advantage or wants to live a selfish life. Instead, each one lives for the others. No longer are we many, but one in Christ. We long that in us who strive against our own nature, God's nature may be seen and that through our unity the world may recognize the unity of the Father with the Son and the Holy Spirit. And because we are called to witness to the Lord before the people, we feel an urge from God to make known His working, and this we do with joy. All the believers are inwardly assured that this is God's holy will for His people.

The world does not understand that God works in the heart. So God has given men the outer witness of the Scriptures. He commands, "Gather all my holy people, those who have made a Covenant with me by sacrifice." David said, "I am in the community of all who fear Thee and keep Thy commandments." In Isaiah we read that all man's produce and gain "shall be dedicated to the Lord; nothing shall be

Ezek. 11:19

John 17:21

Ps. 50:5

Ps. 119:63

Isa. 23:18

hoarded by anyone. All the products of the citizens of Tyre shall be the Lord's and be used to feed the hungry and clothe the aged."

This community was practiced by the Church of Christ in Jerusalem. And wherever men's hearts are moved by the Spirit of God to live together, the same practice is mirrored in their brotherly love and care. Each one, by the grace given him, wants to serve and help the other, not just for the sake of that other one but so that all are guided by the Word of truth and drawn to the Lord. This is what believers in every generation have longed for, as it is written:

> How lovely is Thy dwelling place, Ps.
>   O Lord of hosts, 84:1,2,
> My soul longs, yea, faints 4,10
>   for the Lord.
> My heart and my body rejoice
>   in the living God.
> Blessed are they who dwell
>   in Thy House and praise Thee
>   unceasingly.
> For one day in Thy courts is better
>   than a thousand anywhere else.

I would rather be a doorkeeper in the
  House of the Lord than dwell
  in the tents of the godless.

Ps.
122:1-3
I rejoiced when they said to me,
  "Let us go up into the
  House of the Lord!"
Our feet will stand within thy gates,
  O Jerusalem!
Thou art built as a city that is
  firmly bound together.

Ps.
26:3-8
Thy goodness is before my eyes.
I walk in Thy truth
And do not sit with false men
  or have fellowship with the
  malicious.
I hate the company of evildoers
  and will not sit with the wicked.
I wash my hands in innocence
  and go about Thy altar,
So that I might hear the songs
  of thanksgiving
  telling all Thy wondrous deeds.
O Lord, I love to dwell
  in Thy House and the place
  where Thou art honored.

Ps.
87:1-3
On the holy mountain stands the City
  He founded;

the Lord loves the gates of Zion
more than all the other dwellings
of Jacob.
Wonderful things are said of Thee,
thou City of God.

So all the faithful are eager to go where
the chosen ones are gathered. There God's
glory shall be loudly proclaimed. As the
wise Sirach points out, each animal con-
sorts with its own kind, and men cleave to
their own sort. "Birds of a feather flock
together, and so will truth return to those
who practice it." Ecclus. 13:16; 27:9

Many people are moved by the truth
and long to surrender themselves to it, and
God is adding daily to the number of those
who are saved. But among them are some
lukewarm souls. These people are twisted
in their consciences. They resemble Judas,
who was one of the apostles but later
betrayed his own Master for money. They
act under false pretenses. They despise the
truth and then shamelessly slander what
they never understood. In this way they
destroy themselves and spread so many
lies about us that it would take forever to

Acts 2:47; 16:5

Matt. 26:14-16 Mark 14:10,11

investigate all their accusations. They act like the adulterous wife, who deserts her husband and becomes a whore. She spreads all kinds of evil about him as her reason for leaving him, though he has treated her honorably and done only good to her.

This is exactly what these impudent people do. After having left the truth they are not ashamed of spreading falsehoods and claim they have been cheated of their belongings. Most of these people did not bring anything with them anyway; they would not even have had the means to come into this country if we had not helped them. And if some of them did have considerable possessions when they came, they all freewillingly gave them up (as they declared) for the support of widows and orphans and all needy people. Before doing this they were given enough time to get to know the truth and to understand our Orders and our whole way of life. When we did not want to baptize them right away but asked them first to grow into the communal life, many of them pleaded with tears to be accepted

James
1:27

into the Church community of Christ.
They assured us that from then on they
would serve not themselves but the Lord
and His people, seek not their own benefit
but the good of the whole Church community, and give all their goods for the
support of the poor and needy.

When we finally accepted them because
of their constant pleading, we made it
clear that they were giving not only their
possessions but their whole life to the
Church. So in answer to their longing and
request, we accepted the things they had
brought. From then on the goods were no
longer theirs but belonged to the Church
community; for among us no one has Acts
anything of his own. All we possess is used 4:32-37
to support the children, the old, the sick,
and the needy.

If anyone owned property and gave it
up in this way, you yourselves will
recognize that we have no obligation
before God or men to return anything to
him. And if he had nothing of his own, he
neither lent us anything nor gave us
anything for safekeeping. It is therefore
our request to you, for your own sake, not

to commit an injustice by judging in ignorance. When complaints of this sort come to you, accusing us of treating someone unjustly, we ask you not to accept them immediately but also to hear our side, as the law demands.

We hope you will hear good reports about us too and that you realize all these complaints come more from envy and deceit than from a desire for justice.

We hear that the guilds are also complaining bitterly about us, saying we snatch the bread right out of the workers' mouths. We only know that we work very hard to give each one good value for his money. The report of our conscientious labor has spread through the land and made us very popular, so that many want us to work for them. To God alone be honor for this! So even if people complain about us, it will not make us slacken in our efforts. We want to deal justly with all men and support ourselves by hard work and honest labor, not to please men but to please God in Heaven.

Gal.
1:10

This is a short summary of our position on the questions that we heard are of most interest to you. In case anyone wants to know more about these or other articles of our belief, we are sending with this letter a confession of faith that covers all the main points of our belief and way of life.[1] It is concise but thorough and witnesses to the godly way of life. It is the rule we seek to obey in order to follow the Lord our God with a clear conscience. We also want to work conscientiously here in Moravia, giving good and useful service and causing no harm. All we ask is to be allowed to stay here with our children, with our old and sick ones, for the short time we still have to live.

We feel that God has not brought us here without a purpose. He has allowed an amazing measure of religious freedom to exist in Moravia. Neither king nor emperor has power to rule in matters of faith, but each man is free to serve God

[1]Assumed to be Peter Rideman's *Rechenschaft*, written in 1540. (Beck, p. 172, footnote 1) Peter Rideman's *Rechenschaft* was printed as early as 1545 in German and again in 1565. It was first published in English translation in 1950 and is now available from the Plough Publishing House.

according to his beliefs. Should anyone misuse this freedom and refuse to give wholehearted obedience to God and His truth, he will have to face his Judge.

By completely disregarding that freedom, the King is misleading you Lords of Moravia to threaten the believers with death and to scatter them. His boldness drives you to scorn that freedom and to sin by laying violent hands on God's peaceful people. A certain timidity has come over you and taken away your courage to withstand the King and oppose his commands. Even now you are ready to lay hands on the Lord's people and scatter them far and wide at the King's instigation.[1]

We know that we are promised freedom nowhere if we live faithfully in the truth

[1] Ferdinand I (1503-1564), 1521 Archduke of Austria, 1526 King of Bohemia and part of Hungary, 1556-1564 Holy Roman Emperor, was determined to enforce Catholicism in the countries under his dominion. The provinces resented interference from Ferdinand's government in Vienna. With agreement from Vienna, they elected provincial governors from their midst, but as Ferdinand I was never certain whether his orders were carried out, he often sent them instead to the Bishops.

In Moravia, the Anabaptists were at first protected by the nobles (Catholics) who profited greatly from the flourishing communities on their lands. Ferdinand I personally attended a provincial diet in 1535 to enforce his orders and prevail on the reluctant lords to expel the Anabaptists.

and are obedient to God. We must suffer persecution. That alone will show what is in our hearts; it will show whether or not we have chosen God as the highest good. All those who wish to live a godly life in Jesus Christ will be persecuted. Those who turn away from evil will become the prey of evil men. But woe to anyone who lays hands upon the innocent, for as said above, they are laying hands upon the "apple of God's eye." And though God may chastise His people, at the end He will throw the rods in the fire and burn them. As the Lord says: "When I have finished all my work on Mount Zion and Jerusalem, among my people, then I will punish the arrogant boasting of the kings, their haughty pride." And Paul says the same thing when he writes, "God deems it just to repay with affliction those who afflict the believers."

1 Cor. 4:11-13

Matt. 5:11,12 John 15:20 Isa. 59:15

Zech. 2:8

Isa. 10:12

2 Thess. 1:6

We are said to be a great number of people living together, a multitude—some talk of thousands. We want to let you know that there are about two thousand of us, not counting children, living in about twenty different places. At some places there are many people, at others less, depending on the work available at each one. At Schäkowitz, where such an outcry was raised, there are quite a few people, but many of them are children, and many are old or sick and cannot work much. We are not writing this because we are ashamed of them and would rather ignore them. On the contrary, we wish there were many thousands more seeking nothing but to serve God alone.

Because of the injustice of all the false accusations about us, we thought it was only fair to tell you the truth, to write you a brief statement of the facts. In doing so, we entrust ourselves to the care and protection of our almighty Father.

At the same time we warn you and all men not to raise your hand against the believers and so bring on yourselves the judgment of God. For it is true that the more tyrannical the nations become, the closer draws their punishment. It is also true that wherever compassion has been shown to God's people, the country and its inhabitants have been spared for the sake of His Church. This is what happened when the Turkish invasion was the tool of God's punishment. The Turks overran Austria but did not invade this country. That was not because Moravia was more able to withstand them, but only because God was protecting His people and for their sake protected this country. For the same reason God spared the land only for Lot's sake when He destroyed Sodom and Gomorrah with fire and brimstone. Gen. 19:15-29

From these examples it is clear that if you raise your hand against God's peace-loving people and scatter them, He will not spare you. So beware that you do not load more guilt upon yourselves. For your sakes we have to tell you this.

Amen.

APPENDIX A

Jakob Hutter
c. 1500-1536

Johann Loserth gives the following account of
Jakob Hutter's life:

It is a false assumption to consider the
simple and unlearned hatmaker Jakob
Hutter the founder and beginner of the
Anabaptists in Tirol; for the Anabaptist
movement had long been thriving when
Hutter entered it. But it is certain that
none of his predecessors or successors in
the eastern Anabaptist movement equaled
him in importance; for none was so
successful in creating and reforming. He
not only afforded the cause a strong

support when it had begun to waver in the extremely difficult times; he was also the founder of that peculiar organization which preserved itself in Moravia with its communal character to the end, the founder of the Brotherhood named for him, which still has shoots growing on the American continent. It is therefore easy to understand when the *Geschichts-Bücher* of the Anabaptists speak of him in highest praise, beginning, "At that time one came, by the name of Jakob."

He was a native of the hamlet of Moos near St. Lorenz near Bruneck in the Puster Valley of Tirol. Scantily educated by the school at Bruneck, he went to Prague [Prags, Tirol] to learn hatmaking. Then he began his extensive journeys for the sake of his trade and finally settled at Spittal on the Drau in Carinthia. In Klagenfurt he probably made his first contact with the teachings of the Anabaptists, which became so significant for his inner development. He was never in Silesia or Bavaria and learned of Gabriel Ascherham and his Silesians only when in 1529 he came to Moravia to find a quiet place for his little congregation. It is not known when he was baptized, but after he had "accepted the covenant of grace of a good conscience in Christian baptism with true resignation to lead a godly life and God's gifts were richly felt in him, he was chosen and confirmed in the Service of the Gospel."

In this position he first traveled through the Puster Valley, Tirol. One of the first small congregations he headed was that at Welsperg. Here his adherents assembled alternately in the house of his relative, Balthasar Hutter, and that of Andreas Planer, a scythe-smith. At the latter place he baptized ten persons on one day. The government had word of this "synagogue" in May 1529 and now ordered Christoph Herbst, the sheriff at Toblach-Welsberg, to surprise and seize the Anabaptists. Some were captured, but Hutter and others escaped. The statements of the prisoners were sent to Innsbruck. They gathered from them that Jakob Hutter, a real leader, "baptized the others for money"; what is meant is that each had to make a contribution to the common treasury.

Though the leader escaped this time, the authorities seized his sister Agnes in 1529. She had a short time previously been pardoned, but had at once returned to the Brotherhood. By this act her sentence was already pronounced. The persecution of the "pious in the land" gradually grew intolerable. On every side one saw the blood of the martyrs and the burning stakes, prisons filled with captives, children forsaken and starving at home, with never a ray of hope except in God.

Then some recalled that the Lord of Hosts had gathered a people in His name in the city of Austerlitz in Moravia. The elders decided to send brother Jakob and Simon Schützinger to them to gather information. After hearing his favorable report the Brotherhood in Tirol decided to join the one in Moravia. Hutter appointed his co-worker Georg Zaunring to lead them, and sent one small group after the other to Moravia. Most of them were members of Blaurock's orphaned congregation (Blaurock had been burned at the stake on September 6, 1529, at

Klausen).[1] Singly and in groups, driven by the persecution prevailing throughout the land, the Anabaptists sought the road to Moravia. There was hardly an alternative. The government pointed out in a letter to King Ferdinand in Vienna that for two years hardly a day had passed in which Anabaptist matters had not come up in the council; "and more than 700 persons have been in part executed, in part expelled, in part have fled into misery, who left their property as well as their children behind." All the rulings were of no avail. "These people not only have no horror of punishment, but even report themselves; rarely is

[1]Georg Blaurock, Conrad Grebel, and Felix Manz were the first three to practice believer's baptism (1525). Blaurock continued his evangelical work in the valleys of Tirol. Here Jakob Hutter came to know the Anabaptist movement, and soon became one of its leaders. "According to the testimony of Christoph Herbst of Toblach on May 26, 1529, Jakob Hutter was already 'an Overseer of the others.' So he must have been in contact with Georg Blaurock during the summer of 1529, although Georg Blaurock was active a little farther south than Jakob Hutter. . . . In August 1529 Georg Blaurock was again in the neighborhood of Klausen, where his powerful ministry was ended by his arrest on August 14, and his life came to an end on September 6. During the autumn of this year, Jakob Hutter traveled to Moravia as the generally accepted representative of the Tirolean brothers, so we can assume that this mission of his must have been at least planned with the agreement of Georg Blaurock." (Eberhard Arnold, p. 49 f., footnote 3)

one converted; nearly all only wish to die for their faith."

Here Hutter worked on without fear. In the early summer of 1530 he wrote a letter about it to Moravia. But while he was devoting all his energy to the care of his brethren at home, conflicts arose in Austerlitz in the winter of 1530, which threatened the very existence of the congregation, and finally split it into two hostile camps. The causes of this division were misapplication of Church regulations by ordained ministers, irregularities in Church discipline, mismanagement of possessions, lack of tact in critical cases, the ambition of certain individuals, all of which Reublin sharply criticized in his letter to Pilgram Marpeck of 1531.

A part of the congregation then went to Auspitz, but not without having sent a messenger to Hutter, asking him to investigate the difficulty. The Austerlitz group did the same. Therefore Hutter and Schützinger went back to Moravia, investigated "where the error in dispute lay, and found that the Austerlitz group was most to be blamed." After they had settled the quarrel they returned to Tirol, but had to go back to Moravia the next year to establish order once more. At this time Anabaptism came to full bloom in Moravia. From Silesia, Swabia, the Palatinate, and Tirol came a long procession to Moravia.

At this time begins the struggle of the Tirolean Anabaptists for their existence. The year 1533 marks the climax of the persecution of the Anabaptists in Tirol, for the government neglected no measures for their suppression. Special efforts were made to capture Hutter, "who had brought so many people of the district into the sect." But no one was found who could claim the reward offered for his capture. When it was finally decided by the Anabaptists in the Gufidaun region that tyranny had reached the highest degree, so that it was no longer possible for them to live there, Hutter was commissioned to go to Moravia to prepare a new home for the emigrants.

On August 11, 1533, he arrived in Auspitz with one companion. The majority of the Brotherhood there wished

to accept Hutter, who was known for his
energetic action, as their leader, but this
ran counter to the wishes of their current
leaders, Schützinger, Philipp, and Gabriel.
And yet in view of the continued friction
in the congregation, there was imperative
need for clear-sighted leadership. These
leaders had shown themselves incapable of
energetic execution of original Anabaptist
doctrine. They had no clear grasp of
true brotherhood, and tended to cling to
family ties, which were incompatible
with unadulterated Anabaptist doctrine.
Reublin's complaints about the education
of the children, the difference in the treat-
ment of the members in food and clothing
and in respect, show how inadequate their
leadership was.

Hutter's attack on the problem was
different. The court records relate that he
distributed to the poor the money
collected from the members: "This
Jakob," say the *Geschichts-Bücher*, "also
brought a temporal gift, a sweet sacrifice,
a little food, so that they could repay their
debt of the time of need." More important
to Hutter than choice by the lot was inner

awakening: "The Holy Spirit called him for leadership." He could not escape it. It was his duty to reform matters. He stated this emphatically in his first address before the Brotherhood. After a few days he began the improvements. But he was opposed by Schützinger, who claimed the office of leadership on the strength of his election by the Brotherhood. He therefore betook himself to Gabriel in Rossitz. "He wanted to see clearly whether the people wanted him as their leader or not. To be quiet and not perform the duties of his office he was not free to do before God. If he was not needed, he would move on, wherever God directed him."

The Hutterites now formed a new Brotherhood and Hutter was able to lead them with a firm hand. The *Geschichts-Bücher* say, "He put the true Church in pretty good order by the help and grace of God; hence we are still called the Hutterites." The loss created by the withdrawal of Schützinger and of the dissatisfied elements under his leadership was replaced by fresh additions from Tirol. In a letter written immediately after the separation Hutter named 120 to 130 persons who had come in the last few weeks. The reports he sent from the Church at Auspitz to Tirol caused a veritable mass migration of Anabaptists to Moravia; they came singly and in groups.

To provide for the continued growth, Hutter was compelled to look about for new homes; thus in the same year (1533) Schäkowitz, a half mile south of Auspitz, was settled. The only serious difficulty arose from their relationship with the adherents of Philipp, his opponent, who also lived in Auspitz. The additions from Tirol continued in increasing numbers; even Tirolean noblemen like Sigmund von Wolkenstein made pilgrimages to Auspitz. At the beginning of 1534 the movement was general among the Anabaptists of Tirol. Soon the government was shocked by reports that nearly all the valleys in the Sterzing district were full of them; three leaders had come from Moravia and were agitating in the region of Schwaz. Almost at the same time it was rumored that Hans Amon was planning "to send the people he had misled from the true faith in the

Puster Valley and other places" to Moravia in the coming spring. Although orders continued to be issued to guard the boats on the Inn River, nevertheless the emigrants managed to get to Moravia. It can be imagined what pleasure the report—false, to be sure—created in Brixen, that Hutter and Amon had been seized in Linz. A considerable number of brethren were captured at Hohenwart in Lower Austria; to them Hutter wrote a long letter of consolation. Here in Auspitz, he said, there was also great tribulation. In Tirol there were no longer many brethren. These, too, were preparing to go to Moravia under the untiring leadership of Hans Amon.

But in Moravia affairs had also taken a turn for the worse for the Anabaptists. The blow that was to strike them here had long been in preparation and was in essence the consequence of the events that had taken place in Münster; but it did not materialize until 1535. The Moravian Diet, which was attended by Ferdinand I in person, acceded to his wish to have all Anabaptists expelled (see p. 180, footnote 1).

In vain they lamented that they were being driven illegally from their possessions. No one in Moravia had ever had cause for complaint to the government. But if the sovereign or the feudal authorities demanded tribute or taxes they were willing to pay as much as they were able, if they were only permitted to keep their work and their religion. A petition did indeed reach the court, but was disregarded. Marshal Johann von Lipa, who took them into his protection, was threatened with the disfavor of the king. They had to move out into wretched poverty.

Hutter took his bundle on his back, as did his assistants; the brethren and sisters with their children went in pairs. "They were thus," their *Geschichts-Bücher* relate, "driven into the fields like a herd of sheep. Nowhere were they permitted to camp until they reached the village of Tracht in the possessions of the Lord of Liechtenstein. There they lay down on the wide heath under the open sky with many wretched widows and children, sick and infants." In touching words Hutter wrote to the governor Kuna von Kunstadt:

"Now we are camping on the heath, without disadvantage to any man. We do not want to wrong or harm any human being, not even our worst enemy." (See Letter IV.) This merely resulted in greater efforts to capture Hutter.

Now the Brotherhood itself insisted on Hutter's leaving. He committed his office to Hans Amon and bade his relatives farewell; with pain and grief they saw him leave. Those remaining scattered, some here and some there. A little group settled at Steinabrunn in Lower Austria, some on the estates of lords who did not feel bound by the latest decree. Hutter's ideal, "the Brotherhood," was now broken up, but preserved itself in numerous small groups. Many who were unable to endure the trials of the brethren returned home.

Thus many returned to Tirol. There, led by Hutter, they began anew their evangelization. "The ungodly tyrants," he writes to his forsaken Church, "do not yet know that we are here. God grant that they do not find it out." But even before Hutter appeared in Tirol the cry resounded on every hand, "Anabaptists from Moravia are roaming through the country!" Orders were at once issued for their arrest. During the period from early September to the end of November 1535, Hutter wrote three letters to the brethren in Moravia. In one he wrote, "God has again set up a Church. His people are increasing in numbers daily. The harvest is nearly ripe, but the laborers are few"; in another he spoke of the "raging" of the foe. "They threaten with hangmen and bailiffs." "The Sodomite sea is raging madly. I fear it will not come to rest until the pious Jonah is cast into it." He warned the Brotherhood of treachery.

Hutter's last letter, written shortly before his capture, indicates the great danger hovering over him. With so many enemies he could not hope to remain undiscovered. When he and his wife were spending the night in the home of Hans Steiner, a former sexton, at Klausen, they were surprised by the clerk of Seber and the city judge Riederer, and together with Anna Steiner of Sankt Georgen and the aged wife of the sexton they were taken to the neighboring episcopal fortress of

Brandzell. The capture of Hutter was immediately reported to Brixen and from there on December 1 to Innsbruck, where the news was received with pleasure and orders were issued to transfer Hutter to Innsbruck, for he was not an ordinary prisoner but a leader; the hearing of his wife was to take place before the city judge in Klausen. In Hutter's bag were found letters from Hans Amon in Moravia, which were sent to Innsbruck with the statements of the arrested women.

Hutter was then taken to Innsbruck under strong escort on December 9 in severely cold weather and was cross-examined two days later. The attempts made by Dr. Gallus Müller to convert him were fruitless. Even if he had recanted, his tragic fate would not have been averted, for the final decision of Ferdinand I was, "We are determined that even if Hutter should renounce his error, we will not pardon him, for he has misled far too many, but we will let the penalty which he has merited so abundantly take its course." He was to be closely questioned on his activity within and without the land, and

precautions taken not to let him be
replaced with other leaders from Moravia;
orders to this effect had already been sent
to Moravia.

Apparently it was expected that Hutter
would ultimately be converted, but this
was not achieved—neither by the torments
of the rack nor by the barbarous whip-
ping. Hutter was firmly resolved not to
yield in matters of faith nor to betray his
brethren. He endured every degree of terrible torture and "remained steadfast to the
end." The sentence condemned him to
death by fire. The court had doubts concerning the advisability of a public execution; but the king would not consent to
having him executed with the sword in the
quiet of dawn; he insisted on a public
execution at the stake. He died on
February 25, 1536, and in the words of
Hans Amon, "He gave a great sermon
through his death, for God was with him."
A trusted brother was at once sent to
Moravia by the orphaned Brotherhood to
bear the news of his departure to the
brethren there.

Hutter's wife had meanwhile been
examined in Brandzell, but as the official

report says, persisted "in her obstinate foolish opinion." She was transferred to Gufidaun where a learned and tactful man was assigned to convert her from her error, but she escaped before he arrived. Two years later she again fell into the hands of the government and was executed at Schöneck.

Hutter's death was commemorated in song by his adherents. But his old opponents carried their rancor beyond his death. Only Philipp Plener, also an opponent in Hutter's Moravian period, gave a juster verdict: "No one provided so faithfully for the people in temporal or spiritual matters as Hutter. Never was he found unfaithful. Through him the Lord gathered and preserved His people." In general his brethren recognized his service to the Moravian Anabaptists in reestablishing discipline and order, confirming the "community" in opposition to destructive private ambitions, cleansing it of impure elements, and averting the abuses that brought dissolution of the groups in other places.[1]

[1]Johann Loserth, "Hutter, Jakob," *M.E.II*, pp. 851-853, slightly adapted.

The Hutterian history book gives a moving account of Jakob Hutter's death:

The priests, in their evil, vindictive passion, thought they would try to drive the devil out of him. So they had him dipped in ice-cold water and then taken into a hot room, where he was beaten with rods. They lacerated his body, poured brandy into the wounds, then set fire to it and let it burn. They tied his hands and feet and gagged him again so that he could not denounce their wickedness. Then they put a plumed hat on his head and took him into the house of their idols, because they knew how much he detested it. So they mocked and ridiculed him in every way they could think of.

A heroic fighter for Christ, he was unwavering in his faith. Therefore he was sentenced to death. After suffering much at the hands of evil men, the brood of Caiaphas and Pilate, he was burned alive at the stake.

As he was being led to the fire he said, "Now come here, all you disputers, and let us prove our faith in the fire. This fire will not harm my soul any more than the fiery furnace harmed Shadrach, Meshach, and Abednego."

He was executed in the presence of a large crowd of people, who were witnesses of his faithfulness and courage. This happened at Candlemas, on the Friday before Lent, in the year 1536.[1]

[1]A.J.F.Zieglschmid, ed., *Das Klein-Geschichtsbuch der Hutterischen Brüder*, pp. 40-41.

APPENDIX B

Historical Background to Letter II

The events reported in Jakob Hutter's second letter are one chapter in the struggle that led to the establishment of the Hutterian Church. Some more detail may help the reader to grasp the sequence of events and understand why Hutter used such strong language in this letter.

Beginning in 1525, the Anabaptist movement spread rapidly through the Hapsburg territories of southern Europe. In 1528 Jakob Wideman and a group of Anabaptists (about two hundred adults) left the town of Nikolsburg in Moravia. They were no longer tolerated there because they refused to carry swords or pay war taxes. They gave up all rights to personal property and started living in full community at Austerlitz. In Tirol also there was a movement of Anabaptists, which Jakob Hutter joined in 1529. The brothers soon recognized Jakob's faith and dedication and appointed him to the Service of the Word. Having heard about the group living together at Austerlitz in Moravia, the Anabaptists in Tirol sent Jakob Hutter, Simon Schützinger, and several others to visit them.

Thus Jakob Hutter visited Moravia for the first time in 1529. He saw with great joy that the Austerlitz group was already putting into practice the teachings of Jesus according to the New Testament, and he had the humility to unite with them on behalf of his congregation in Tirol. He left in peace and unity with the Austerlitz group and went home, where the news of the uniting was greeted with great thankfulness to God.

Two other Anabaptist groups started living in community in the vicinity of Austerlitz at about the same time. Gabriel Ascherham, coming with a group from Silesia, established a community at

Rossitz in 1527. Philipp Plener also came to Rossitz in 1527 with a group from Swabia, Hesse, and the Palatinate, and lived with the Gabrielites for a while. Gabriel even gave the leadership over to him. But later Gabriel disagreed with Philipp's actions and took back the position. In 1529 Philipp and his people moved to nearby Auspitz. They were no longer united, but they called themselves brothers and their basic teaching and organization were the same.

Jakob Hutter sent several groups of Anabaptists from Tirol to join Wideman's group at Austerlitz. Among the brothers who arrived were Georg Zaunring and Wilhelm Reublin. In the winter of 1530 Reublin brought complaints against Wideman before the gathered Church in Wideman's absence. He and Zaunring objected to some of Wideman's teaching and to how he had handled certain situations. Wideman had threatened some single sisters that if they did not marry according to his suggestions, he would have to get heathen girls for the young men. Some members had kept money and bought what they wanted for themselves. These and other disorders had gone unchallenged by Wideman.

When Wideman returned, they talked about these deviations privately and before the Church, but Wideman and his followers did not let Reublin speak in the meetings. They did not come to peace, and in the end Reublin and Zaunring with about 150 members were forced to leave. They moved to Auspitz (some sources say on January 8, 1531), fully aware that they would face extreme poverty but determined to live in total community of goods and depend on God alone. They formed a new community in the same town where the Philippites lived.

Both Wideman's group and the break-away community sent messengers to Jakob Hutter in Tirol for help in this crisis. This was to be his second journey to Moravia, again with Simon Schützinger. Just shortly before their arrival, it was revealed that Reublin himself had secretly kept back money. Jakob Hutter looked into this situation with the elders when he arrived, and Reublin was excluded, which Reublin himself recognized as right and just. Then Hutter heard the causes of the split from both sides and found that the Austerlitz group was most at fault: they had excluded innocent members, tolerated freedom of the flesh and private property, and allowed marriages with unbelievers. He challenged them to repent, but they would not listen to him. From that time on the so-called Austerlitz brothers were not considered part of the Church. Jakob Hutter and Simon Schützinger appointed Zaunring to care for the Church at Auspitz as Shepherd or Servant of the Word, and they returned to Tirol.

Not long afterward however Zaunring had to be excluded too, because when his wife committed adultery, he kept it secret, excluding, forgiving, and reaccepting her, all without the Church. Now the Church at Auspitz was without a Servant. They sent for Jakob Hutter again, who came for the third time with Simon Schützinger, around Easter 1531. Jakob encouraged the Church, saying they had done rightly to exclude Zaunring. Simon Schützinger was appointed to take Zaunring's place. (Zaunring later repented and was re-accepted.)

Soon after that, Jakob and Simon united their group with Gabriel's and Philipp's. The three groups—Gabriel Ascherham's at Rossitz, Philipp Plener's at Auspitz, and Simon Schützinger's also at Auspitz—agreed that none would make any major decisions without the advice of the others. Jakob then returned to Tirol.

The three communities grew because of the severe persecution in Silesia, Swabia, the Palatinate, and Tirol. Around this time, Simon's community may have had 1400-1500 members, Gabriel's 1200, and Philipp's 500-600. The three communities lived in peace until 1533, when the great split occurred that Jakob Hutter writes about in this letter. This is what happened.

Jakob Hutter arrived in Moravia for the fourth time on August 11, 1533. He came with a group of believers who were fleeing from Tirol. He was welcomed by Simon Schützinger, the elders, and all the people with great joy and asked if he would help care for the flock.[1] He preached the next Sunday and said among other things that he would help to set right anything that was wrong in the House of God. After a few days he made a beginning, but Simon objected. Jakob wanted to know why and said he was compelled by God to carry out his calling and could not be inactive. If they did not want him, he would move on. Jakob Hutter then went to Rossitz to tell Gabriel his dilemma.

In Jakob Hutter's absence, Simon spoke to his two Stewards against Jakob, declaring his determination to stay in the leadership without Jakob's help. When

[1]A letter sent ahead by Hans Amon to his fellow countryman and brother, the Steward Leonhart Schmerbacher, was intended to pave the way for Jakob Hutter in Auspitz: "I ask you particularly in regard to our brother Jakob that you accept him. I write this in confidence, to caution you and all brothers and sisters: When brother Jakob comes to you, I hope he will serve you as your Elder (or Overseer) and that the brothers and sisters will put their trust in him. On the other hand, some might be narrow-minded and reluctant to accept him. I ask you to watch out that this does not happen and that no bitterness takes root among the Servants of God." This is how the movement in Tirol under the leadership of Hans Amon represented that Jakob Hutter be recognized as Servant of the Word and Elder of the people of God, although earlier Simon Schützinger had been appointed Servant of the Word in Moravia under Jakob Hutter's leading.(Eberhard Arnold, p. 75, footnote 1)

Jakob came home from Rossitz, Simon faced him with the question of what he was going to do next.[1] In a talk with Simon and the elders, Jakob said he wanted to ask the Church whether they needed him or not, because he felt he must carry out the task God had given him. But Simon said that God had given the care of the people to *him*, that *he* had been chosen by lot to be their Shepherd or Servant of the Word. He insisted that he wanted to do it alone, even when the elders said he should serve together with Jakob.

When Gabriel and Philipp were drawn in, Gabriel accused Jakob of trying to take the Shepherd's Service over from Simon. Jakob asked, "How would you like it if one of you left his community in someone else's care while on a journey and then on coming home had to stand back?" After much discussion among the elders, Jakob again requested that the matter come before the whole Church.

[1]This attitude to Jakob Hutter, who had brought him to Moravia and appointed him to the Service, reveals that Simon was straying from the way. There is no other explanation for his disunity with the apostolic Servant of the Word. (Eberhard Arnold, p. 76, footnote 5)

The following Sunday Jakob told the gathered Church about all they had discussed. Simon spoke, saying he wanted to keep his Service. Gabriel spoke long on Simon's behalf, and then the Brotherhood was asked to speak. Two or three said that Simon should continue and Jakob should help; another said one was as good as the other, but Simon cut him short. The Steward, Leonhart Schmerbacher, agreed that one was as good as the other, but that for the sake of peace, love, and unity, Jakob should let Simon take first place. Everyone said yes, yes. Someone added that Simon was good enough by himself. Then Gabriel asked Jakob if he would accept the decision of the Brotherhood. He replied that he would have to consider it before God and discuss it with the elders and Servants before he could answer. Gabriel refused to talk with him. Everyone went home very sad. Some went to comfort Jakob, who was deeply grieved.

When the Church met again on Tuesday, Jakob said he still felt that God had led him to be their Shepherd. For the sake of love, peace, and unity he would accept the Church's decision, though not for the sake of justice.

Two weeks later Simon fell sick. Jakob took the meetings and on the second Sunday spoke about true community. Again there was grumbling against him among several brothers. Shortly afterward, it was discovered that when Georg Fasser had handed in his family's possessions to the Church, his wife had kept back some money. Then Jakob felt uneasy and wondered if Simon Schützinger's wife had also kept some money. With the support of the elders, he organized a search of all the houses, beginning with his own. And she did indeed have money hidden away. Simon admitted that he had known about it and even brought out forty florins more that were hidden under the roof. The elders were all very shocked. The next day, October 5, 1533, they laid Simon's unfaithfulness, greed, and deceitfulness before the Church. The brothers and sisters were very pained and wept, but they excluded him according to the Word of God, as he himself recognized to be right.

Then Jakob said to the Church that they should reconsider what they had done by choosing Simon to be their Shepherd and rejecting Jakob as ungifted for that task. Now they had no Shepherd. Jakob also said he was not sure whether he should serve them, because they had so despised the Word of God. But he asked them to pray to God that He might give them a faithful Servant.

They prayed day and night for a week. They also sent two brothers to Gabriel at Rossitz to ask his advice, and he suggested that Jakob Hutter be given the Service. While the Church was gathered in prayer, all became of one heart and one mind and accepted Jakob as their Shepherd and Servant, as a gift from God. On October 12, they confessed before God and to Jakob Hutter that they had done wrong in giving precedence to Simon, the deceiver. They recognized that Simon was not the Servant of God they thought he was, and they asked for forgiveness. God forgave them. Then the Word of God was fruitful among them; peace, love, and the fear of God flourished. The wicked were put out of the Church, and believers were taken in.

Two weeks passed. On October 26, 1533, when the Church was gathered before daybreak to hear the Word of God, Philipp and Gabriel and Blasius Kuhn and Peter Hueter walked unannounced into the meeting.[1] Many were alarmed, but the elders and Servants welcomed them. Jakob Hutter asked them what they had come for. They said they had some questions to the Church: why David Böhem and others had been excluded and why it was now said that Simon Schützinger's appointment had not been from God. There was a lot of talk back and forth, one accusing the other of lying. Everyone was shocked and dismayed, and no one any longer knew who was right. But at last Philipp and Gabriel exposed the deceit in their hearts. Philipp called Jakob Hutter a liar and accused the Brotherhood of making an idol of him and worshiping him. At that there was great turmoil in the Brotherhood, and they cried out, "That is a lie!" When Philipp was revealed as a liar and slanderer, he tried to gloss it over and take back what he had

[1]See Letter II, p. 24.

said. Philipp and Gabriel maintained that they had nothing against the Church, only against the leaders. They suggested that a small group of brothers, chosen from all three Brotherhoods, should decide who was in the right. No one answered them, so they left.

However, the next Monday Jakob's Brotherhood sent four brothers to Philipp and four to Gabriel to explain why it had taken the steps in question. Philipp did not receive them as brothers but slandered them, accusing them of excluding Simon out of envy and hate, accepting Georg Fasser into the community for the sake of his money, and worshiping Jakob Hutter. The four brothers protested. They went home and reported to the Church.

During the following weeks, the three groups sent delegates back and forth, trying to arrange a meeting to discuss the problems and to overcome the differences and make peace. Jakob Hutter and his Brotherhood were willing to take part in such a meeting and accepted the conditions laid down by Philipp and Gabriel. They were even willing to have the three groups meet without the three leaders. Philipp and Gabriel and their followers, however, raised objections to every attempt at reaching an agreement.

The struggle ended on November 22, 1533, with complete separation between the three communities. The three groups never reunited, and in 1535 they were scattered by severe persecution.

APPENDIX C

Authorship of Letter IX

Our translation of Letter IX was made from a typescript in the Woodcrest Archives (EAH 159, Part I, pp. 223-269). This typescript is a copy of a manuscript lent to Eberhard Arnold in North America in 1930 and returned in 1933. The manuscript had been copied from early codices by Johannes Hofer of Buck Ranch Bruderhof, Milford, Alberta, in 1904. It bears the following heading: "A letter (*Sendbrief*) from Jakob Hutter on behalf of the whole Church and Brotherhood to the Lords of the land of Moravia, sent around the year 1545." It concludes: "End of Jakob Hutter's epistle and letter."

Eberhard Arnold describes this document as "An important old confession of faith of Jakob Hutter and Peter Rideman of 1535-1545," thus allowing for the possibility that Peter Rideman either wrote it in 1545 or sent an existing confession of faith by Jakob Hutter. Other scholars also ascribe this confession to Peter Rideman. (See Robert Friedmann in *Hutterite Studies*, p. 267.) Johann Loserth says, "Of Hutter's writings only his eight epistles have been preserved." (M.E. II, p. 854)

Beck includes a shortened form of this rare document without ascribing it to anyone. (Beck, pp. 169-173)[1] The Hutterites themselves looked upon the authors of such documents as the spokesmen for the whole Brotherhood. Perhaps that is why this document has been handed down without being clearly credited to one individual. The Spirit that prompted Jakob Hutter and Peter Rideman was the same Spirit that animated the whole Brotherhood.

---

[1]Beck's sources are listed as Codex Nr. 215 in the Domkapitel library in Pressburg (Bratislava) and Codex G.I. VI 31 in the Primatial library of Gran (Esztergom).

APPENDIX D

The Hutterian Stand on Marriage and Divorce

Readers of German will find Dr. Fischer's historical background to Jakob Hutter's letters very helpful. His attempt to give an account of the inner life, however, as it comes to expression in such Church actions as baptism, Lord's Supper, and marriage, makes it clear that he inevitably sees the life as an outsider. His citations from old sources are sometimes misleading. At the request of some representatives of the Hutterian Church we would like to correct the statement on marriage and divorce quoted by Dr. Fischer on page 64 of his book. It is to be found in a letter written in 1607 by a certain Lorentz Grötzner, who was clearly not a member of the Hutterian Church, though not unsympathetic.

The quotation says, "If the one partner

should move away while the other stay [that is, if one married partner should leave the communal life of the Hutterian Church], the latter cannot marry unless the one who moved away marries."[1] This was not the attitude of the Hutterian Church in Jakob Hutter's time nor is it today. The Hutterian Church has always stood by the words of Jesus about marriage and divorce. (Matt. 19) A member of the Hutterian Church, even one whose partner has left the Church community (or never joined it), recognizes his or her marriage bond until death, regardless of what the unfaithful partner may do.

The great Confession of Faith of 1545 by Peter Rideman, still held to by the Hutterian Church today, says:

> Marriage is a union of two, in which one takes the other to care for and the second submits to obey the first, and thus through their agreement two become one, and are

[1]In F. Mencik, "*Ein Schreiben über die Wiedertäufer,*" *Zeitschrift des deutschen Vereins für die Geschichte Mährens,* Vol. 15, 1911, pp. 364-372.

no longer two but one. But if this is to be done in a godly way they must come together not through their own action and choice, but in accordance with God's will and order, and therefore neither leave nor forsake the other but suffer both ill and good together all their days.[1]

[1] Peter Rideman, pp. 97-98.

BIBLIOGRAPHY

Arnold, Eberhard, editor. *Kleines Geschichts-Buch, Erster Teil.* 1932, (Unpublished, annotated edition of the "Small Chronicle," never completed.)   [Eberhard Arnold]

Beck, Josef, editor. *Die Geschichts-Bücher der Wiedertäufer in Österreich-Ungarn.* Nieuwkoop: B. de Graaf, 1967.   [Beck]

Fischer, Hans. *Jakob Huter: Leben, Frömmigkeit, Briefe.* Newton, Kansas: Mennonite Publication Office, 1956.   [Fischer]

Friedmann, Robert. "Jakob Hutter's Last Epistle to the Church in Moravia, 1535," *The Mennonite Quarterly Review.* Edited by Harold S. Bender. Goshen, Indiana: Mennonite Historical Society, January 1960.

_____. *Hutterite Studies.* Edited by Harold S. Bender. Goshen, Indiana: Mennonite Historical Society, 1961.

225

Loserth, Johann. *Der Anabaptismus in Tirol.* Vienna: Kaiserliche Akademie der Wissenschaften, 1892. [Loserth]

The Mennonite Encyclopedia. Edited by Cornelius Krahn. Scottdale, PA: Mennonite Publishing House, 1955-1959. [M.E.]

Phillips, J.B. *The New Testament in Modern English.* New York: Macmillan Company, 1958.

Rideman, Peter. *Confession of Faith: Account of Our Religion, Doctrine, and Faith,* 2nd ed. Rifton, New York: Plough Publishing House, 1970. [Peter Rideman]

Wolkan, Rudolf, editor. *Geschicht-Buch der Hutterischen Brüder.* Macleod, Alberta: Hutterian Brothers, 1923. [Wolkan]

Zieglschmid, A.J.F., editor. *Die älteste Chronik der Hutterischen Brüder.* Philadelphia, PA: Carl Schurz Memorial Foundation, 1943.

_____. *Das Klein-Geschichtsbuch der Hutterischen Brüder.* Philadelphia, PA: The Carl Schurz Memorial Foundation, Inc., 1947. [Zieglschmid]

INDEX

Adige Valley, 13, 14, 45, 80, 135
Agnes (sister of Jakob Hutter), 188
Amon, Hans, 16, 42n, 46, 63, 194-200
Arnold, Eberhard, xii-xiv, 189n, 211n, 212n, 219
Ascherham, Gabriel, 23, 24, 31, 36n, 63n, 186, 192f, 206-218
Auspitz, 10n, 11n, 13, 23n, 28n, 36n, 42n, 49, 51, 63n, 78n, 159, 190, 191, 194, 195, 207-210, 211n
Austerlitz, 5, 6, 10n, 11, 36n, 188, 190, 206, 207, 209

Bärbl, 47
Blaurock, Georg, 188, 189n
Böhem, David, 35, 36n, 216
Both, Hans, 36n
Brähl, Ursula, 46
Braitmichel, Kaspar, 10

Brandzell, 199, 200
Brixen, 137, 154, 155, 156n, 195, 199
Bruchsal, 24n
Bruneck, 186
Bucovic, 5, 6
Bühler (Philler), Christel, 116

Casper, 134
Christel, 6, 10
Christina, 17

Eggenburg, 16n, 49n
Enn, 8n

Falkenstein, 10n
Fasser, Georg, 46n, 47, 63, 214, 217
Fasser, Ursula (wife of Georg), 46f, 214
Ferdinand, King, 66-73, 114, 170, 180,
    189, 195, 196, 199, 200
Fleischhacker, Hans, 10

Gabriel: *see* Ascherham, Gabriel
Gabrielites, 207
Glaser, Bastel, 49n
Governor of Moravia: *see* Kuna von
    Kunstadt, Johann
Grebel, Conrad, 189n
Gredl, 17
Greiffenburg, 126
Griesbacher, Wilhelm, 63

Griesinger, Offrus, 16, 42n, 46, 63
Grötzner, Lorentz, 221
Gsäl, Waltan, 17
Gufidaun, 17n, 191, 201

Hän, Georg, 6, 10
Hänsel, 119, 122, 128f, 134, 140
Herbst, Christoph, 187, 189n
Hofer, Johannes, 219
Hofer, Joseph, xiii
Hofer, Zacharias, xiii
Hohenwart, 49, 195
Holitsch, 10n
Hueter, Peter, 18, 24, 216
Hutter, Balthasar, 187
Hutter, Katharina (wife of Jakob Hutter),
    78n, 198f, 200f

Inn River, 195
Inn Valley, 14, 18, 45
Innsbruck, 116, 187, 199

Jembach, 47
John of Leyden, 168n

Käls, Jeronimus, 46n, 84, 134, 137, 141,
    156
Käls, Traindel (wife of Jeronimus), 134
Kitzbühel, 46n
Klagenfurt, 186

Klärle, 134
Klaus B., 11, 18, 46
Klausen, 189, 198, 199
Kleinsasser, Joseph, xiii
Kränzler, 84, 134
Kuhn, Blasius, 24, 216
Kuna von Kunstadt, Johann, Governor of Moravia, 65, 66, 196

Leyden, John of, 168n
Liechtenstein, Lord of, 196
Linz, 195
Lipa, Johann von, 196
Lorenz, 10
Lüsen, 154-156

Manz, Felix, 189n
Marbeck, Gredl, 46
Marpeck, Pilgram, 190
Marx, 35
Maurer, Kuntz, 15, 20
Maxwell Bruderhof, xiii
Meier, Paul, 126
Meier, Peter (judge at Vintl), 125
  daughter of, 119, 125f
Michel, 75, 85, 104f
Moos, 186
Müller, Gallus, 199

Münster, 168n, 195
Münsterites, 168, 170

Nändl, 99f, 119, 127, 134
Nieder, Martin, 116
Nikolsburg, 10n, 205
Nikolschitz, 36n

Paul (Meier), 126
Pergen, 10n
Philipp: *see* Plener, Philipp
Philippites, 208
Planer, Andreas, 187
Plattner, Hans, 10
Plener, Philipp, 23f, 31, 36n, 63n, 192,
    194, 201, 207-218
Prague (Prags, Tirol), 186
Purst, Katharina: *see* Hutter, Katharina
Puster Valley, 8n, 14, 18, 45, 46, 80, 84,
    135, 186, 187, 195

Rattenberg, 28n
Reublin, Wilhelm, 36n, 190, 192, 207-209
Rideman, Peter, 179n, 220, 222
Riederer, 198
Rockport Bruderhof, xii, xiii
Rosedale Bruderhof, xiii
Rossitz, 23n, 24, 193, 207-215
Rüpel, 17

St. Lorenz, 186
Sankt Georgen, 198
Schäkowitz, 10n, 194
Schmerbacher, Leonhart, 63, 211n, 213
Schmidt, Christel, 103, 119, 128, 140
Schneider, Gilg, 35, 36n
Schöneck, 125
Schuster, Lorenz, 10
Schuster, Michel, 15, 20
Schützinger, Simon, 23n, 28, 31, 35, 36n,
      188, 192f, 206-217
Schwaz, 194
Seber, 198
Spittal on the Drau, 186
Steinabrunn, 10n, 197
Steiner, Anna, 198
Steiner, Hans, 198
Sterzing, 84, 116, 194
Stoffel, 17, 134

Tauffers, 154
Toblach-Welsberg, 187, 189n
Tracht, 65, 196
Traindel (wife of Jeronimus Käls), 134
Trässenhofen Bruderhof, 24n
Trieste, 10n

Valt, 17

Vienna, 180n, 189
Vintl, 125
Voit, Peter, 13, 16, 49n

Walser, 127, 134
Welsperg, 187
Wideman, Jakob, 36n, 205, 207f
Wolkenstein, Sigmund von, 194

Zaunring, Georg, 36n, 188, 207-210
Zentz, 17
Zimmermann, Wölfl, 103

BOOKS FROM THE PLOUGH PUBLISHING HOUSE

Confession of Faith by Peter Rideman in 1540-1541, 304 pages

Brotherly Community, the Highest Command of Love. Two Anabaptist Documents of 1650 and 1560 by Andreas Ehrenpreis and Claus Felbinger, 150 pages

The Early Anabaptists by Eberhard Arnold, 64 pages

The Early Christians after the Death of the Apostles, edited by Eberhard Arnold, 484 pages

Inner Land: A Guide into the Heart and Soul of the Bible by Eberhard Arnold, 588 pages

Also available in 5 small volumes:
Vol. 1 *The Inner Life*
Vol. 2 *The Struggle of the Conscience*
Vol. 3 *The Experience of God and His Peace*
Vol. 4 *Light and Fire and the Holy Spirit*
Vol. 5 *The Living Word*

Torches Together: The Beginning and Early Years of the Bruderhof Communities by Emmy Arnold, 240 pages

Foundation and Orders of Sannerz and the Rhön Bruderhof by Eberhard Arnold, 80 pages

Love and Marriage in the Spirit by Eberhard Arnold, 260 pages

In the Image of God: Marriage and Chastity in Christian Life by Heini Arnold, 184 pages

Salt and Light: Talks and Writings on the Sermon on the Mount by Eberhard Arnold, 344 pages

God's Revolution: The Witness of Eberhard Arnold, edited by the Hutterian Brethren and John Howard Yoder, Paulist Press, 1984, 232 pages

Living Churches: The Essence of Their Life
by Eberhard Arnold
Vol. 1 *Love to Christ and Love to the Brothers*,
36 pages
Vol. 2 *The Meaning and Power of Prayer Life*,
64 pages

When the Time Was Fulfilled: On Advent and Christmas
by Eberhard Arnold, Emmy Arnold, Christoph
Blumhardt, and Alfred Delp, 256 pages

*Freedom from Sinful Thoughts: Christ Alone Breaks the
Curse* by Heini Arnold, 136 pages

*Seeking for the Kingdom of God: Origins of the Bruderhof
Communities* by Eberhard and Emmy Arnold, 308 pages

*Eberhard Arnold: A Testimony of Church Community
from his Life and Writings*, 120 pages

*Children's Education in Community: The Basis of
Bruderhof Education* by Eberhard Arnold, 68 pages

Living in Community: A Way to True Brotherhood
by Heini and Annemarie Arnold, 24 pages

Why We Live in Community by Eberhard Arnold, 24 pages

COMPLETE LISTING OF PLOUGH BOOKS
SENT ON REQUEST

Names and addresses of communities of the Hutterian Brethren:
Woodcrest, Rifton, NY 12471, USA
Pleasant View, Ulster Park, NY 12487, USA
New Meadow Run, Farmington, PA 15437, USA
Deer Spring, Norfolk, CT 06058, USA
Pembrook, Ipswich, SD 57451, USA
Darvell, Robertsbridge, E. Sussex TN32 5DR, United Kingdom
Crystal Spring, Ste. Agathe, Manitoba ROG 1YO, Canada